ASSUMED
CHRISTIANITY

ASSUMED CHRISTIANITY

"I never knew you…"

A.D. Sikes

Published by Acknowledge Publishing LLC   AC v11b

ISBN-13: 978-1-7340384-0-8

CONTENTS

Introduction

At this point, 7,722,982,923 people occupy this earth. We are all here for a reason, but it seems there are 7.7 billion different understandings of what that is. Governments of the 195 countries throughout the globe try to lead people in a variety of directions, and religions do the same. Various world religions guide close to 84% of the world population with the remaining people considering themselves to be nonreligious/secular/agnostic/atheist. The point here is that there are countless ideas and beliefs regarding the purpose and direction for this earthly life, so it is no wonder life is so chaotic.

How does all of this relate to Christianity? Most Christians believe we are on the right track and generally hope and pray that the other billions of people will join us. However, that is not the primary topic of this book. Instead, this book addresses the fact that the current 2.3 billion self-proclaimed Christians have many different understandings of what it means to be a Christian. While that may not matter to some of us, it does to the one who does matter – Christ Jesus!

It matters to Him and ultimately to us as professed Christians because Jesus tells us that: *many are called but few are chosen* (Matthew 22:14 ESV). It matters because if we are called, we can be assured that we are among the few who have been chosen before we meet Jesus on that judgment day. It matters because if we are chosen, our new life in Christ begins on earth as we grow closer to the glory of God.

EXAMINE YOURSELF

Because Jesus tells us that many professed Christians are erroneously assuming they have been chosen, this book is an invitation to assess your relationship with God and be assured of your eternal salvation. Because so many people are being influenced by the lies and deceptions of the world, the Bible tells us, "*Examine yourselves to see whether you are in the faith; test yourselves...*" (2 Corinthians 13:5).

Part 1 describes the situation where many people are erroneously assuming their eternal salvation. We see Jesus' prophesy about this and then see how the lies and deceptions of our world are causing many people to think they are good with God. Fortunately, we can see that God provides the truth, allowing us to see through our assumptions and truly believe and receive Jesus as Savior.

Part 2 takes us to the Word of God to learn how we can be assured that we are among the *few* who are chosen and adopted into the eternal family of God. We see that we all begin life on what Jesus describes as the Broad Road to destruction that is currently crowded with billions of lost people. Everyone on that road is destined for eternal separation from God unless we accept God's call to truly believe and receive Jesus. We see what it means to answer His call and see the supernatural changes that takes place as we pass through the Narrow Gate onto the Narrow Road to life. We also see from the Bible that no efforts on our part contribute to our rebirth as a new creation in Christ. It is truly by God's grace alone that we are chosen and transformed at that point into a new creation and adopted child of God.

Part 3 describes the new life of a person who has been reborn as a new creation in Christ and adopted into God's eternal family. Regardless of our physical age, knowledge of the Bible and record of church attendance, as new children of God we must grow and mature spiritually and we see how that happens. We also see examples of new life in Christ from the first generation of Jesus' disciples who follow Jesus as Lord.

Part 4 provides a brief summary of the Bible for us to allow us to replace our assumptions with truth of God and His plan and purpose for this earthly life. Without that truth, even with good intentions, people end up worshipping a god of their own creation rather than the one true God. Also, by knowing the truth of God's plan and purpose for this life, we find peace and understanding as we deal with the chaos that surrounds us and those we love.

Ensuring you have received God's Gift of eternal salvation is the first priority. If you are already assured of your rebirth as a new creation in Christ, you may be able to discover your next step as you turn to God to become the masterpiece that He created you to be. None of this can be done on our own, but only with the grace of God. We are told to draw near to God and He will draw near to us. Let us answer His call to do that.

STUDY GUIDE

This study is designed with seven sessions, but we recommend one or two extra sessions depending on the needs and interests of the group.

Before Each Gathering

Do the following before each small group meeting:

- Read the chapters associated with each lesson (described on the next page). As you do this, underline points of interest and list comments and questions that come to mind.
- Read the questions at the end of each chapter and don't rush to answer. Allow yourself time to hear God speak to you.
- Even if you do not read everything prior to meeting with your group, attend anyway and learn from the discussion.

At Each Gathering

- Begin with a prayer to hear God and His truth, screening out the lies and deceptions of the enemy. Pray that your assumptions will be exposed and replaced by His Truth.
- At the first meeting, take the opportunity for each person to briefly summarize their spiritual background – acknowledging that everyone is in a different stage of spiritual maturity and relationship with God.
- Allow general conversation about the lesson topic. Then, turn page-by-page through the chapter(s) to discuss anything that anyone has highlighted or questioned. If there are questions or comments that suggest future research, begin a list of those questions and topics.
- Discuss questions at the end of each chapter.

Remember that the process of growing closer to God is a journey rather than a time-specific lesson, so allow this study time to be fruitful and enjoyable. Also remember that people are often in very different points in their relationship with God and at different stages of spiritual maturity. Think of this study as a way to hear God speak to the needs of each person.

Part 1 – THE SITUATION

The situation was announced by Jesus more than two thousand years ago to describe what will take place at the final judgment of many people who profess to be His followers. Jesus is raising a warning flag that He will not recognize *many* people who profess to be Christians. Furthermore, He tells us that we will not be allowed to explain our misunderstandings and assumptions. Jesus then says those self-professed Christians will be turned away from the presence of God for eternity. There will be no appeal at that point. This is explained in Jesus' words in Matthew 7:21-23.

Next, we examine why so many people are erroneously assuming they are good with God. We know that assumptions are a part of daily life, but we see that Satan uses subtle lies and deceptions to create false assumptions of the truth about God. Fortunately, we also see that God provides the absolute truth upon which we can know Him and live for His glory and purpose.

Because there will be no appeal when we meet Jesus at judgement, now is the time to turn to God to receive and believe Jesus as the way, truth and life.

1. Not Everyone Who Says

The situation is now, and you are part of it. Imagine that throughout the world, at the very same moment, Jesus communicates directly with every person who professes to be a Christian. At work, school, home, or at a sporting event you receive the equivalent of an Amber Alert on your phone. You may be in the middle of a business meeting or taking a final exam. If you are watching a movie or TV or playing games on your device, the screen goes dark, and a message appears. If you are driving, the music is interrupted, or the radio turns on with a voice that attracts you to listen. If you are sleeping or amid hospital surgery, you receive a dream message that is as clear and vivid as though you were awake. Regardless of your primary language, the message is delivered with precise translation. However, if you do not profess to be a Christian, you are not aware that Jesus' one-minute announcement is happening:

> "I am interrupting the life of every person who professes to believe and follow Christ Jesus as your Savior. I speak this brief message and warning because of my love for you. As I look ahead to the judgment day, as it is now, many of you will be turned away from eternally living with the Father,

Son, and Holy Spirit. Many professed Christians will be surprised and dismayed because they are mistakenly assuming their eternal salvation. In desperation, they will present their stories of many things done in my name. While it is not my wish, unless they truly believe and receive me and are reborn as adopted children of God, I will turn them away without appeal and say, 'I never knew you.'

"But it doesn't have to be that way. The opportunity is now, so please accept this invitation and be assured that I will be welcoming you into God's heavenly home for eternity. When you truly believe and receive Me as Savior and Lord, you are reborn as a new person and then grow to become the person God created you to be. You will be assured and will not doubt your salvation when that happens. I gave My life for you to have this opportunity, so please, accept My invitation for the glory of the Father. Christ Jesus."

SAID BEFORE

The fact is, that broadcast has already happened. Jesus delivered that message to all of us when He said: *"Not everyone who says to me, 'Lord, Lord,' will enter the kingdom of heaven, but only the one who does the will of my Father who is in heaven. On that day many will say to me, 'Lord, Lord, did we not prophesy in your name and cast out demons in your name, and do many mighty works in your name?' And then will I declare to them, 'I never knew you; depart from me, you workers of lawlessness'* (Matthew 7:21-23 ESV).

More than two thousand years ago, Jesus said those words as part of His Sermon on the Mount to multitudes of people who were following Him and considering themselves to be His disciples. Jesus continues to speak this to us today and it is eternally worth our attention. If this came from anyone else, it would be easily dismissed as contrary to what we assume it means to believe in Jesus as the Savior, but these are His words!

"Not everyone who says to me, 'Lord, Lord,' will enter the kingdom of heaven. Jesus gets right to the point. Of course, our first reaction might be to dismiss this entire verse as applying to people of other religions, atheists and the like. Christians can also point to those among them who never go to church or turn to God only when desperate. It's easy to assume that Jesus is not addressing us.

"On that day... Jesus refers to judgment day when the eternal destiny of each person is announced.

"many ... The fact that He said "many" rather than "some" or "a few" is also notable. Furthermore, Jesus was looking into the future and seeing the entire population who consider themselves to be Christians. In other words, many of us.

"will say to me, 'Lord, Lord, did we not... in your name? Every person who considers himself to be a Christian can fill in the blank with examples of good works, charitable contributions, church attendance, and Bible studies. We will be ready to present a convincing case to Jesus on why we should be admitted to heaven. In addition to listing the great things we have done, we will also have reasons for why we did not do more. This earthly life is a challenge, and God doesn't always make it easy, so Jesus should take

all of that into consideration – right?

"And then will I declare to them, 'I never knew you... Jesus states the reason for His judgment, *"I never knew you."* But why does He say that? As God and creator, Jesus knows every one of us. The stakes are high, so now is the time to understand what He is telling us and why.

"depart from me, you workers of lawlessness." Jesus is describing how He will be sentencing these people at the final judgment. Total separation from God for eternity is the ultimate sentence with no appeal. It is also noteworthy that He calls them "workers of lawlessness" because works do not earn salvation. It is by grace alone (and not our works) that we are given new life in Christ. As such, assumed Christians are workers of lawlessness, regardless of their good intentions.

While that may not make sense at this point, it will as you open your heart and mind to learn the truth of God's Word. Submit to the Word of God in the Bible and welcome Him to draw near to you and help you understand what He means to believe and receive Jesus in faith.

IT'S ALL ABOUT LOVE

You may be tempted to toss this book aside and refer to many other verses and Bible stories that describe the loving God who is calling us to be with Him in heaven. But it is because He is the loving God that Jesus tells us now – before we get to that irreversible point at judgement. Fortunately, as long as we are still breathing, and regardless of what we have done in the past, we can accept His call to be reborn as a new creation in Christ. *But whoever loves God is known by God* (1 Corinthians 8:3).

Also consider how Jesus must feel about having to dismiss many people from His presence for eternity. He allowed Himself to pay the price of sin to provide the opportunity for those people to be adopted into God's family, but they never submitted to Him as Savior and Lord.

HOPE

At that future judgement, there will be no hope for people who refuse to surrender and come close to Him in this earthly life today. Jesus will say He does not know them as believers who have received Him, and He banishes those people from the presence of God for eternity.

But now we have hope, and He is calling us to be transformed into people He knows. Regardless of what has happened in the past or now, God is calling us to truly believe in Jesus as Savior and receive Him as Lord of our life going forward. We do not have to pay the price (nor can we do it anyway) for all the wrongs we have done, regardless of how bad or good we think we have been. The price for the justice of our sin has lovingly been paid by God through the suffering and death of Jesus – but only for those who truly believe and receive Him.

NOW OR LATER

You can put it off until sometime in the future, but that is a risk with eternal consequences. Who knows what might happen on your next trip to the store or walk around the block? Plus, it is another bad assumption that life with Christ will not be as good as the life you are living now. The opposite is true. Living in Christ is immeasurably better than life without Him and God's divine resources. So, now is the time to receive Him and be known by Him.

DISCUSSION AND REFLECTION

1. For the past few years, what were your thoughts on how God will be judging you? Will He be leaving room for assumptions and misunderstandings? Will you have the opportunity to present your case?

2. Discuss Matthew 7:21-23 and describe how it relates to what you have been thinking and believing before beginning this study. Take it word-for-word if you need to, because understanding how to deal with this is the heart of this book.

3. It is easy to dismiss this warning as not relating to us, or promise to address it in the future. Discuss the risk/rewards of dismissing or postponing this assessment of your relationship with God. Do you fear that your life might change or that you might uncover something you don't want to admit?

2. Assumptions

Sometimes, we don't know what we don't know. We think, speak, and act based on our assumptions about a situation, but often we don't know the full story or the true story. That results from casual efforts to know the truth, or because the truth is disguised with lies and deceptions. When that happens, everyone involved must deal with the consequences. Sometimes our assumptions work out, but often they don't. Financial investments, business decisions, career choices, and personal relationships are some examples. We can make excuses for our words and actions based on our misunderstandings and assumptions, but life forward is never the same, even if we are forgiven.

Forgiveness is another topic that we can assume to understand. We can see from God's Word that He offers forgiveness, but the offer eventually expires as described in Matthew 7:21-23, *"I never knew you; depart from me..."* for eternity. Because many people are refusing to acknowledge their assumptions and replace them with God's truth, they will suffer the consequences throughout eternity.

WHY WE ASSUME

Why do we say and do so many things based on assumptions rather than truth? In some situations, there is urgency, so we must immediately act based on what we assume to be true. That's when experience, general knowledge of the truth, and our relationship with God can keep us out of trouble. Another common reason for going with assumptions is that acknowledging the truth may interfere with whatever we want to do. We know there could be adverse consequences, but we go-ahead for immediate satisfaction, pleasure, control, or rage that we are determined to experience. It seems like our nature drives us to think and act based on our emotions, expectations, and desires, which are often not aligned with God's will. We also know, from the Word of God, that Satan is our enemy whose purpose is to attract us away from God with lies and deceptions. If we do not understand why God allows life to be the way it is, we often come up with assumptions to help us cope. We assume because we do not know the truth or because we do not want to accept it.

MANAGING ASSUMPTIONS

As a practical matter, we cannot stop to evaluate the validity of everything we assume, or we become paralyzed from living. We live in a fast-paced world, and we need to learn how to best deal with the fact that we often have incomplete information, false information, or both. The Project Management function in business recognizes the potentially devastating impact of assumptions on large projects and has developed a methodology for managing them. Assumptions are identified along with their constraints and risks as part of the formal project management process. While there is a cost to do this, the result is always better than not acknowledging the assumptions. The question then becomes, how can we do this in our daily lives without having to analyze everything we do and say? How can we base our words and actions on the truth rather than on erroneous assumptions?

The answer is the Holy Bible, which is the truth. Both the Old and New Testaments provide the truth we need as background to act and react to situations we face every day. As we grow to know God through His Word and the Holy Spirit, we become empowered to understand how to handle each situation and opportunity in the best way. By knowing the truth, we can avoid assumptions that are harmful to others and ourselves.

True believers also have another resource for knowing God's truth. Because Jesus no longer lives on this earth, we may assume His timely advice is not available. The truth is that we are better off that Jesus is not here now as the only light of truth among 7+ billion people. He said it this way: *But I tell you I am going to do what is best for you. This is why I am going away. The Holy Spirit cannot come to help you until I leave. But after I am gone, I will send the Spirit to you.* (John 16:7 CEV).

DISCUSSION AND REFLECTION

1. Think of some of your past assumptions that have resulted in adverse consequences. Did you assume because you couldn't know the truth, didn't take the time to know, or because you wanted to go ahead anyway?

2. Are assumptions about daily life less important than making assumptions about God? Is there a difference?

3. Do you sometimes choose to think, speak, and act without wanting to know the truth and possible consequences?

4. Would you be willing to allow everything you think, say, and do to be directed by truth rather than assumptions? What exceptions and why? How might that change your life?

3. Truth

"*What is truth?*" the powerful Pontius Pilate sarcastically responded after Jesus told him why He came to this earth: "*In fact, the reason I was born and came into this world is to testify to the truth*" (John 18:37). Pilate didn't want to be dealing with the situation. He told the Jewish leaders who brought Jesus to him, "*Take him yourselves and judge him by your own law*" (v31). However, because the Jews did not have the authority to execute anyone, they went to the Roman government to permanently get rid of Jesus. They weren't asking for justice, but rather for the verdict they wanted. Pilate was caught in the middle, and it appears that he tried to let Jesus argue His way out of the sentence that the Jews were demanding:

Pilate then went back inside the palace, summoned Jesus and asked him, "Are you the king of the Jews?" "Is that your own idea," Jesus asked, "or did others talk to you about me?" "Am I a Jew?" Pilate replied. "Your own people and chief priests handed you over to me. What is it you have done?" Jesus said, "My kingdom is not of this world. If it were, my servants would fight to prevent my arrest by the Jewish leaders. But now my kingdom is from another place." "You are a king, then!" said Pilate. Jesus answered, "You say that I am a king. In fact, the reason I was born and came into the world is to

*testify to the truth. Everyone on the side of truth listens to me."
"What is truth?" retorted Pilate. With this he went out again to the
Jews gathered there and said, "I find no basis for a charge against
him. But it is your custom for me to release to you one prisoner at
the time of the Passover. Do you want me to release 'the king of the
Jews'?" They shouted back, "No, not him! Give us Barabbas!"* (v 33-
40).

Jesus' answer at that crucial moment was not unlike a closing
argument at a trial. After all the things Jesus had already done and
was about to do, why did He talk about truth? He could have said,
"I came to seek and save those who are lost" (Luke 19:10); or, "To
be an example of how to live here on earth" (Matthew 20:28); or,
"To do the will of the Father" (John 6:38); or, "To be a light shining
brightly in a world of darkness" (John 12:46); or, "So people can
have abundant life" (John 10:10); or, "To proclaim the good news
about the Kingdom of God" (Mark 1:38); or, "To pay the price for
the sins of the world" (John 12:27); or, "To demonstrate the love,
mercy, and grace that God has for us" (1 John 4:10); or, "To give
people the opportunity for eternal life with Him" (John 3:16).
Instead, Jesus said: *"The reason I was born and came into this world
is to testify to the truth."* It is like saying that truth encompasses all
other reasons for His coming to earth. But Pilate shrugged it off as
most people would today.

Jesus knew what Pilate's reaction would be and knew the pain,
suffering, and death that would soon follow. Nevertheless, Jesus
stayed with His truth answer because He is truth: *"I am the way and
the truth and the life. No one comes to the Father except through me*
(John 14:6).

FINDING TRUTH

Knowing and acting on the truth is a big problem today as it was two thousand years ago when Jesus lived on this earth. However, for true believers of Jesus, it can be done. The answer is not found in one religion or another, but rather in Jesus and the Word of God in the Holy Bible. Some Christian churches and pastors are aligned with the Word of God, but others are not.

Most people are worshipping false gods. The enemy has profiled God with so many lies and deceptions that most people, including many professed Christians, have no idea who the one true God is. Even world religions, some Christian denominations, and individual churches have redefined God so that people are worshiping false gods and don't know. So, begin by asking God to reveal some of His never-changing attributes as you pray and study His Word.

So, while this book can get you started or restarted in the right direction to be assured of your eternal salvation, that assurance can only come directly from God as you draw close to Him. We are told in James 4:8, *Come near to God and he will come near to you,* so we have God's word on it. It also matters not who we are now or what we have done in the past because God calls us to begin anew. However, drawing near to God requires faith because we do not know how life will change as a result – and He promises it will. We have things we want to do, existing commitments, and friends we want to keep. All of that and more are at risk when we draw near to God. But not drawing near to God is the approach taken by the many people that Jesus will be dismissing for eternity when He will say, *"I never knew you."*

THE BIBLE

God gives us His truth in the Bible so we have no excuse for making erroneous assumptions about God and His plan for this earthly life.

In the beginning, when only two people existed, and the earth was perfect, God's directions came from His audible words that were clearly stated. *Then God blessed them and said...* (Genesis 2:16). His direction was simple: Enjoy everything to the fullest, take care of this place, allow Me to lead you, and never attempt to take over. Today we have a more comprehensive resource in the Bible, but God's direction is the same. The details in the Bible are necessary because billions of people have created so much chaos by not following His simple instructions.

Even with God's revelations, commandments, and rules of practice for how we should live, life continues to go astray. The bottom line is: too many people still don't know or have given up knowing the true purpose of this earthly life journey. Most people, even many professed Christians, do not read the Bible and are not listening to God relate His message to their lives.

OUR PERSONAL LINK TO GOD

The fact that the Bible continues to exist over time is a tribute to the one true God. The fact that it relates to each of us is also amazing. To those of us who have a new life in Christ, God speaks through the words of the Bible and the Holy Spirit. We come to the Word of God from every nation and culture, from every season of life, with every possible need, and God's Word speaks to every one of us. Jesus describes it this way: *"I have much more to say to you, more than you can now bear. But when he, the Spirit of truth, comes, he will guide you into all the truth. He will not speak on his own; he will speak only what he hears, and he will tell you what is yet to come. He will glorify me because it is from me that he will receive what he will make known to you. All that belongs to the Father is mine. That is why I said the Spirit will receive from me what he will make known to you"* (John 16:12-15).

However, the Holy Spirit is not present in people who mistakenly assume that Jesus knows them as His disciples. He says in Matthew 13:13-15: *"Though seeing, they do not see; though hearing, they do not hear or understand. In them is fulfilled the prophecy of Isaiah: 'You will be ever hearing but never understanding; you will be ever seeing but never perceiving. For this people's heart has become calloused; they hardly hear with their ears, and they have closed their eyes. Otherwise, they might see with their eyes, hear with their ears, understand with their hearts and turn, and I would heal them.'"* Our ability to know the truth of God's Word begins at the moment we are reborn as new creation in Christ and we receive the Holy Spirit.

As I can testify, it is fortunate that God's call also extends to assumed Christians and others who have not yet believed and received Jesus. Sixteen years ago, in a comfortable work-related situation, I saw this verse written in the far corner of a conference room: *Trust in the Lord with all your heart and lean not on your own understanding; in all your ways submit to him and he will make your paths straight* (Proverbs 3:5-6). It seemed out of place for a production meeting in a paper mill, and it got my attention. Other than me, no one noticed because it wasn't part of any conversation. Having never seen that verse, I was amazed at what it was saying. How could that possibly be true in business and other areas of my life?

I now realize that someone at that facility wrote that verse as an invitation from God to get my attention. Because I could not imagine how it could apply to my life, that verse created a curiosity that led me on a quest to discover and believe the Truth.

RELATIVISM

Without the absolute truth of God's Word, we depend on the relative truth of man. And because that is relative, it is not the truth upon which God expects us to base our lives. For our culture, relativism is the norm because it allows everyone to do his own thing. It is the belief that truth and morality relate to culture and society, rather than being absolute. There is no universal, objective, or absolute truth, according to relativism; instead, each point of view has its relative truth. In other words, most people in our society today assume that each person is entitled to have his own set of beliefs and values as a license for their thoughts, words, and actions. Then, as enough people become convinced they have common perspectives on new practices, leaders define new laws, rights, and moral standards for all people. The cycle continues without consideration for the fact there is an absolute truth to be considered. So, declares our culture, *"what is truth?"*

While this may appear to be a social argument, many professed Christians have beliefs based on assumptions that come from our culture. Studies from the Barna Group confirm this fact that only 17 percent of professed Christians have a biblical worldview. The other 83 percent of professed Christians have beliefs associated with deceptions and assumptions of our culture. It is no wonder that Jesus will be saying, *"I never knew you..."*

Another example of making assumptions is the apostle Peter who reacted to Jesus' foretelling of His pending crucifixion and death. Jesus sharply rebuked him, saying, *"Get behind me, Satan"*. While it may seem like Jesus should have been more considerate, He had a point for all of us to know. He went on to say, *"You do not have in mind the concerns of God, but merely human concerns"* (Mark 8:33).

Jesus' message is that any of us can unwittingly become a spokesman for Satan as we see situations from a worldview perspective, rather than from the truth of God's Word. Perhaps you and I are making assumptions based on the relative views of the world, and Jesus is saying to us, *"Get behind me, Satan."* Think about that for a moment. It is easy to say that it couldn't be me because I believe in Jesus as my Savior and Lord. But, think about Peter who, moments earlier, testified to Jesus: *"You are the Christ."* Jesus is saying that the worldview is based on deceptions and lies that people assume are true. To get beyond that, God's truth must be part of everything we think, do, and say.

It is so easy for us to build our lives and the lives of those we influence on things that are not true from God's perspective, causing us to assume that we are living as He expects us to live. Unfortunately, many people will dismiss His warning throughout their life before being confronted by Jesus at the final judgment. But there is no excuse because God provides opportunities for us to know Jesus as God's truth.

DISCUSSION AND REFLECTION

1. Discuss Jesus' closing argument to Pilate when He said: *"In fact, the reason I was born and came into this world is to testify to the truth."* Is He possibly saying that knowing Him is the only possible way to know God and His truth?

2. How does "truth" relate to Jesus' prophetic warning of Matthew 7:21-23?

3. Why should we not rely exclusively on religion, the church, pastors, preachers, book writers, and friends, as the source of God's truth in the Bible?

4. Discuss the fact that the Bible can become a personal

communication with God. How is that attainable for people who are actively involved in this fast-paced world?

5. Why is it difficult for assumed Christians to understand God's truth in the Bible as described in Matthew 13:13-15? What does it take for us to have a personal communication link with God? Do most people want that personal communication with God, or do they want to continue living without His interference as long as possible?

6. Discuss how the relativism of our culture translates to our assumptions about God. Give some examples.

7. Studies from the Barna Group confirm that only 17 percent of professed Christians have a biblical worldview. Where would you fit into this survey? That statistic seems consistent with what Jesus says in Matthew 7:21-23 where many professed Christians will be separated from God for eternity.

Part 2 – BE ASSURED

The enemy is good at leading us to believe we are good with God based on his deceptive definition of the word believe. Most professed Christians believe that Jesus is the Son of God who died for our sins, rose from the dead, and ascended back to heaven. At the same time, we are led by Satan to assume that a loving God will give everyone the benefit of the doubt at the final judgment. We believe that Jesus will welcome most everyone into heaven as we often hear when people die. However, when we read Jesus' words in Matthew 7:21-23, we may wonder if we can be assured of our salvation. The answer is yes, we are assured when we are reborn as adopted children of God. *And this is the testimony: God has given us eternal life, and this life is in his Son. Whoever has the Son has life; whoever does not have the Son of God does not have life. I write these things to you who believe in the name of the Son of God so that you may know that you have eternal life* (1 John 5:11-13). *The fruit of that righteousness will be peace; its effect will be quietness and confidence forever* (Isaiah 32:17).

So that you may know tells us that we can be assured that we have God's gift of eternal life with Him. There are indicators such as the Fruit of the Spirit. After receiving Jesus and the Holy Spirit, as we grow to know Him, these qualities become part of who we are and how we think, speak and act – love, joy, peace, patience, kindness, goodness, faithfulness, gentleness and self-control. The this is easy to see when we read what God tells us happens when we believe and receive Jesus: *I will give you a new heart and put a new spirit in you; I will remove from you your heart of stone and give you a heart of flesh. And I will put my Spirit in you and move you to follow my decrees and be careful to keep my laws"* (Ezekiel 36:26-27). How can we not know and be assured of our new life in Christ?

To help us understand life before and after receiving Jesus as Savior and Lord, He provides a simple road-trip analogy in Matthew 7:13-14. We see that all people begin life at a disadvantage on the Broad Road to destruction because of the sinful nature we inherit. He tells us that most people never choose to exit that road and never receive new life in Christ. But for those of us who answer God's call, we are led through the Narrow Gate onto the Narrow Road to life where we begin our eternal life as adopted children of God.

4. The Relationship

Some attempts never gel into truly loving relationships because one of the people does not have the full commitment to make it happen. We may blame it on a lack of chemistry, but that's not the case when it comes to a relationship with God. Some of us have grown up thinking that what matters is being good, or at least trying to be. But how good do we need to be? We can always find someone who is more or less good than we are and convince ourselves that God sees it that way. But He does not. Some people think they are good enough and believe that He is a loving God so that everything will work out in the end. Unfortunately, for many people, everything will not work out in the end, according to Jesus in Matthew 7:21-23.

FAITH AND SALVATION

Because of our inherited sinful nature, none of us begin life as part of God's eternal family. Not until we truly believe and receive Jesus are we reborn and adopted as a child of God. But, many professed Christians do not accept the call of God for that new life.

A simple example of that is the criminal who was being crucified for a capital offense alongside Jesus. Following a brief exchange, before they died, Jesus assured the criminal they would be together in paradise later that day. *One of the criminals who hung there hurled insults at him: "Aren't you the Messiah? Save yourself and us!" But the other criminal rebuked him. "Don't you fear God," he said, "since you are under the same sentence? We are punished justly, for we are getting what our deeds deserve. But this man has done nothing wrong." Then he said, "Jesus, remember me when you come into your kingdom." Jesus answered him, "Truly I tell you, today you will be with me in paradise"* (Luke 23:39-43).

That situation shows us about God's gift of salvation and what it means to believe. The criminal expressed his faith in Jesus as God, he confessed himself as a sinner, and surrendered to Jesus as his Savior and Lord going forward. He was forgiven, made righteous as a new creation in Christ, and adopted as a child of God. The relationship was established, and Jesus responded with the confirmation that the man would join Him in paradise later that day. It was profoundly simple. *For by grace you have been saved through faith. And this is not your own doing; it is the gift of God* (Ephesians 2:8 ESV). And fortunately, as I know from experience, we do not have to be facing death to begin new life in Christ.

Compare that situation to the one Jesus describes in Matthew 7:21-23 when He dismisses many professed Christians who had done great things in His name.

HOW TO KNOW

The one criminal on the cross was assured of his eternal salvation because Jesus told him, *"Truly I tell you, today you will be with me in paradise."* Imagine the peace he felt with that personal reply from Jesus. However, since none of us are physically in that position to hear those assuring words of Jesus, can we have the same degree of assurance that we will be with Him in paradise? Fortunately, the answer is yes. First of all, we can be close enough to Jesus to hear Him as He tells us: *Come close to God, and God will come close to you* (James 4:8 NLT). And when we are close to Him, we hear His personal words to us through the Bible and the Holy Spirit: *For the word of God is alive and active* (Hebrews 4:12).

HOW TO KNOW - PEACE

Peace is one indication of a new life in Christ. *And the peace of God, which transcends all understanding, will guard your hearts and your minds in Christ Jesus* (Philippians 4:7). Of course, the world around us and the devil try to divert our hearts and minds from Jesus, but we learn that He is always there to resist the enemy and allow us to have the peace that only He can provide.

HOW TO KNOW - SIN

Another indication is found in 1 John 3:9-10. *No one who is born of God will continue to sin, because God's seed remains in them; they cannot go on sinning, because they have been born of God. This is how we know who the children of God are and who the children of the devil are: Anyone who does not do what is right is not God's child, nor is anyone who does not love their brother and sister.* Although born-again Christians are able to sin and do, we have new divine power to resist temptation. *And I will put my Spirit in you and move you to follow my decrees and be careful to keep my laws.* Our new life in Christ leads us away from sin and toward the fruit of the Spirit. *The temptations in your life are no different from what others experience. And God is faithful. He will not allow the temptation to be more than you can stand. When you are tempted, he will show you a way out so that you can endure* (1 Corinthians 10:13 NLT).

HOW TO KNOW – FRUIT OF THE SPIRIT

Other indicators of our commitment to follow Jesus as Lord are seen as our heart is filled with *love, joy, peace, forbearance, kindness, goodness, faithfulness, gentleness and self-control* as described in Galatians 5:22-23. These are qualities that the Spirit develops in us as our relationship with Jesus matures. As that happens, our life is characterized by the fruit of the Spirit rather than sin.

HOW TO KNOW – TRUE BELIEVERS

We also have many examples of people who show us the fruit of their life in Christ. The apostle Paul is like us in that he did not personally interact with Jesus while Jesus was on earth. Prior to his conversion, he may have been aware of Jesus but there is no record the two had ever met. If anything, it is clear that Saul (his Hebrew name) was an adversary of Jesus because he actively captured and persecuted followers of Jesus. In addition to being a well-educated Jewish leader and defender of the Jewish law, Saul also enjoyed the advantages and influence associated with his Roman citizenship. He was neither a friend of Christians nor a friend of Christ. In a way, before we truly believe Jesus, we are much like Saul because we do not know what we are missing. We can be aware of Jesus and even know much about Him, but still not have new life in Him. Of course, all that changed for Saul when the Spirit of Jesus got his attention on the road to Damascus. It was a dramatic encounter, but Saul still had the decision to accept or reject Jesus' invitation. Lost people get invitations from God to know Jesus, but often dismiss them and go on with life.

The writings of Paul in the New Testament provide vivid examples of how he went all-in to believe and receive Jesus and his life changed dramatically. Later in life, Paul wrote from prison to believers in Philippi, expressing his appreciation for their support. His encouragement to the Philippians gives us a view into the heart and soul of Paul after years of growing closer to God.

I was circumcised when I was eight days old. I am a pure-blooded citizen of Israel and a member of the tribe of Benjamin—a real Hebrew if there ever was one! I was a member of the Pharisees, who demand the strictest obedience to the Jewish law. I was so zealous that I harshly persecuted the church. And as for righteousness, I obeyed the law without fault.

I once thought these things were valuable, but now I consider them worthless because of what Christ has done. Yes, everything else is worthless when compared with the infinite value of knowing Christ Jesus my Lord. For his sake, I have discarded everything else, counting it all as garbage, so that I could gain Christ and become one with him. I no longer count on my own righteousness through obeying the law; rather, I become righteous through faith in Christ. For God's way of making us right with himself depends on faith. I want to know Christ and experience the mighty power that raised him from the dead. I want to suffer with him, sharing in his death, so that one way or another I will experience the resurrection from the dead!

I don't mean to say that I have already achieved these things or that I have already reached perfection. But I press on to possess that perfection for which Christ Jesus first possessed me. No, dear brothers and sisters, I have not achieved it, but I focus on this one thing: Forgetting the past and looking forward to what lies ahead, I press on to reach the end of the race and receive the heavenly prize for which God, through Christ Jesus, is calling us (Philippians 3:5-12 NLT).

Paul's deep relationship with Jesus matured over time with the grace of God and the power of the Holy Spirit. A commitment like that may seem too extreme to someone who has not yet been made into a new creation in Christ. But rest assured, there is no reservation after taking that step forward in faith.

HOW TO KNOW – ABBA FATHER

Some of us are experiencing all of that and more. That said not to boast, but rather to say it can happen. Furthermore, when it does, you know because you become an adopted member of God's eternal family. *So you have not received a spirit that makes you fearful slaves. Instead, you received God's Spirit when he adopted you as his own children. Now we call him, "Abba, Father"* (Romans 8:15 NLT). *Abba* signifies the close, intimate relationship that Father God has with His children, as well as the childlike trust that true believers have with their Father.

When other true believers share their testimonies about their journey with Christ, we see the uniqueness of each. Likewise, we discover that our relationships with God are in different stages of maturity. Furthermore, we are called to help each other to grow because we are not in competition to become better friends with Christ. We know that He has the capacity and desire for every one of us to be best friends with Him.

So, as we allow Jesus to lead us, and we hear Him speak to us through the Holy Spirit as we pray and read the Word of God, we become assured that we are adopted children of God who are maturing to become the masterpiece God created us to be.

SO, WHAT'S NEXT?

If God is calling you to that new life in Christ, you have the next move. The next step is yours to believe and receive Jesus in faith. His invitation to a new life is outstanding and waiting on your faith-filled acceptance. Forget about cleaning yourself up as a prerequisite for responding to His call. Jesus took care of that on the cross. We are foolish to think we are so far gone that we have to first get better before working with God. We are never too bad, regardless of what we have done in the past or are doing now. Furthermore, we cannot repair the damage we have done to ourselves and others, nor do we have the strength to repair ourselves from the damage done by others. Having to make ourselves worthy is a lie the enemy wants us to believe because it keeps us from approaching God. Billy Graham made that point with the song "Just As I Am" that played as he invited people to step forward to believe and receive Jesus.

DISCUSSION AND REFLECTION

1. Why does God allow Satan (the enemy) to deceive some people to erroneously assume they are saved? Will God ultimately excuse misunderstandings because they are based on the deception and lies of the enemy?

2. Do you believe that God allows you to be certain that Jesus knows you as His disciple and a child of God? What are some of the indications that you have that relationship with Him? Will you see these immediately following your salvation?

3. Discuss the characteristics of a good personal relationship with family and/or friends. Are your good relationships all the same? Why?

4. Now, compare your understanding of relationships to the brief exchange that Jesus had with one of the criminals who was being crucified with Him. That saving relationship was established without good works, water baptism, Bible studies and long conversations over time. What does that tell you about what it takes to have a saving relationship with Jesus?

5. Discuss how Saul's saving relationship with Jesus was established.

6. Read Philippians 3:7-14 and see the level of commitment that Paul described. Does Jesus expect that same level of commitment from us, or can we get by with something less?

7. What do you need to do before approaching God and asking Him to adopt you into His family as a child of God? What is Jesus expecting from you?

5. The Broad Road

Knowing about the Broad Road to destruction can help you see why you have the need to be reborn in Christ. *"Enter through the narrow gate. For wide is the gate and broad is the road that leads to destruction, and many enter through it. But small is the gate and narrow the road that leads to life, and only a few find it"* (Matthew 7:13-14). Jesus' words about the Broad Road also help to explain why life is the way it is.

Most Broad Road people are not aware of their path and destination. Some have given up on God because of what is happening, and some do not want Him interfering with their lives. From personal experience, I know that assumed Christians are also unaware they are living on that Broad Road. Attending church, praying merely by rote and desperation, and trying to keep the Ten Commandments are deceptive indicators that we are good with God.

Another reason for not knowing we are on this track is that every one of us is born onto the Broad Road to destruction. Even if we were raised by a family who attended church, God's truth helps to know we need salvation and cannot earn it. Momentum, the multitudes of other lost people, and the lies of the enemy can keep us from knowing we are headed for destruction. Why God allows us to begin like this doesn't make sense until we learn what God's plan is and how it is playing out.

THE OPPORTUNITY

All of us have inherited a sinful nature because Adam and Eve chose to know evil as well as good. However, it is most important to know that the current stage of God's plan provides us with the opportunity to permanently exit from that Broad Road to destruction. *Yes, Adam's one sin brings condemnation for everyone, but Christ's one act of righteousness brings a right relationship with God and new life for everyone. Because one person disobeyed God, many became sinners. But because one other person obeyed God, many will be made righteous* (Romans 5:18-19 NLT) So, without the truth of God's Word, we can only assume that God's plan is for life to be the way it is on the Broad Road to destruction. But when we know His truth, life begins to make sense and we can see His path forward to eternal life with the one true God.

For those lost people still on that Broad Road, the New Testament tells us there is still hope to get off that road, regardless of the damage already done. It is natural to think we have to first get our act together, or that we are too far gone to repair the damage to ourselves and others. The enemy fuels those thoughts to keep us from seeing the truth that Christ Jesus offers the only way to exit from that road with a new life and freedom from the past.

And finally, the danger remains great for people who assume they believe in God and feel that everything will work out in the end. They are satisfied and not looking for the truth. Fortunately, God continues to offer invitations to know the truth.

DON'T WAIT

Jesus is calling assumed Christians to join Him now at the entrance to the Narrow Gate. At the same time, the enemy says you can get to it later, knowing that for many people later never comes. He may also suggest you are too far gone to be forgiven. Don't put it off to prepare because God already knows everything about you and is still calling you to begin anew going forward. He wants to transform you into the person He created you to be. Jesus wants you to ask His forgiveness and believe that you are forgiven by the death of Jesus for your sins. He also knows that your relationships with other people need forgiveness and He promises to help you with those as well. He is ready to make you into a new person with a new life forward. Jesus also knows you need to grow spiritually, just as a child grows into a mature adult. God's invitation is now and Jesus is waiting for you at the Narrow Gate entrance to the Narrow Road of life.

DISCUSSION AND REFLECTION

1. Why is life, for all of us, analogous to a road trip?

2. Explain why every person begins life on the Broad Road to destruction? Also, explain why most people never leave that road.

3. Can you see that, because most people are living on this Broad Road and don't know it, even professed Christians are being deceived as Jesus says in Matthew 7:21-23? Is that a valid excuse?

4. Think of the extremes of people now on this Broad Road. From the most perverted serial killers to "good people" who attend church every Sunday. Are there any limitations of who is permitted to exit from the Broad Road?

6. The Narrow Gate

*" **E** nter through the narrow gate"* is God's call to people who to believe and receive Christ Jesus. That Narrow Gate, which opens onto the Narrow Road to life, never existed before Jesus completed His mission of salvation by suffering and dying for our sins, and then rising from the dead. Jesus paid the price for sins (past, present, and future) of every person who enters through the Narrow Gate. Not only are our sins forgiven, but we are also spiritually reborn as new creations and adopted into God's family for eternity. All of that happens in a moment as a lost person is carried through the Narrow Gate by Jesus.

This road trip allegory allows us to visualize the moment that our life is redirected from the path to destruction onto the path to eternal life with God. On one side of the Narrow Gate is the Broad Road to destruction, on which every person begins their earthly life, and from which most people never leave. That Narrow Gate is the only exit from the Broad Road onto the Narrow Road. It is at the moment of passage when you become assured of your eternal salvation and personal relationship with Christ as a child of God; and what happens at that moment is something only God could orchestrate.

The new believer's sins are forgiven, and because Jesus' sacrifice has paid the penalty for them, this moment is truly the beginning of a new life. *Therefore, if anyone is in Christ, he is a new creation. The old has passed away; behold, the new has come* (2 Corinthians 5:17 ESV). It is the most critical moment of your life because you become a member of God's eternal family for the first time in your life. From that point on, Jesus knows you and always will!

The Bible answers many questions related to this event. Why do assumed Christians not know they are living on the Broad Road to destruction? How can people think they are good with God when they are not? How do we get to the Narrow Gate and what happens when we pass through? Why doesn't God simply forgive us when we ask and give us a new start?

DNA ANALOGY

Forgiveness by God is part of what takes place, but that is not enough to rid us of the permanent damage that was done by sin. Although the Bible does not use a DNA analogy, it helps me to understand why forgiveness is not enough for our eternal salvation. Before sin, Adam and Eve lived with God because they were without sin. However, when sin entered the world, man inherited a sinful nature and was no longer able to live in the presence of God. My analogy is that Adam and Eve's perfect and sinless DNA was altered into a sinful DNA. It was then passed down to their descendants, including all of us today. As such, forgiveness alone is not enough. Furthermore, we do not have the ability to change our sinful DNA back to the perfection that is needed to live with God for eternity. So, we would hope that God could do that, and He can, but not by simply declaring it to happen.

God could not do that because it would violate His very nature as just and righteous. *He is the Rock, his works are perfect, and all his ways are just. A faithful God who does no wrong, upright and just is he* (Deuteronomy 32:4). Because God is just, justice needed to be served to reverse the extreme damage that was done to the nature of man. Man needs to be returned to his original DNA to live in the presence of God, but man cannot do that. Only God could pay the price of justice required to recreate man to his original state of righteous perfection. That justice was paid by the Son of God and the Father who sacrificed His Son for our salvation. Jesus paid the wages of sin as a gift to all of us who choose to believe and receive Him as the only way to the righteous perfection that God created us to be. *"The wages of sin is death, but the free gift of God is eternal life through Christ Jesus our Lord"* (Romans 6:23 NLT). *God made him who had no sin to be sin for us, so that in him we might become the righteousness of God* (2 Corinthians 5:21).

It is a gift from God that we simply must receive. *Yet to all who did receive him, to those who believed in his name, he gave the right to become children of God – children born not of natural descent, nor of human decision or a husband's will, but born of God* (John 1:12-13). God paid the price to create the opportunity for us to return to a righteous DNA state that is required to live in the presence of God. Acceptance of Jesus as Savior and Lord means we are accepting that He paid the price for our sins. If we do not accept a personal relationship with Jesus and His payment for our sins, then we are choosing to pay the price. And because that is not possible, we will suffer the wages of sin for eternity.

REBIRTH

Jesus paid the price and He continues to offer the invitation for lost people to accept His gift of new life. At the moment we believe and receive Jesus as Savior and Lord, we are supernaturally transformed by God into a new creation. We are immediately forgiven, justified, and adopted into God's eternal family. *But when the kindness and love of God our Savior appeared, he saved us, not because of righteous things we had done, but because of his mercy. He saved us through the washing of rebirth and renewal by the Holy Spirit, whom he poured out on us generously through Jesus Christ our Savior, so that, having been justified by his grace, we might become heirs having the hope of eternal life* (Titus 3:4-7 NLT).

As you might expect, you will know you have been reborn as a new creation. And when it happens, you may be moved with the emotion of becoming an adopted child of God for the first time in your life. At the same time, you may wonder what happens next. You feel like a new creation because you are, but the world around you seems to look much the same. It is a wonderful moment, but it can also be confusing to think about how your life may change as a true Christian and follower of Christ Jesus. It is a time of faith to believe that Jesus knows what He is doing as the Lord of your life.

GOOD SOIL

Just as Satan deceived Eve into believing she would not certainly die and would become like God (Genesis 3:4-5), he tries to deceive us about our relationship with Christ. For that reason, we are called to examine ourselves to see if we are in faith of the one true God (2 Corinthians 3:5). Talk to God and hear His call.

Jesus reminds us of Satan's work of deception as He tells the parable of the sower of seeds. *"A farmer went out to sow his seed. As he was scattering the seed, some fell along the path; it was trampled on, and the birds ate it up. Some fell on rocky ground, and when it came up, the plants withered because they had no moisture. Other seed fell among thorns, which grew up with it and choked the plants. Still other seed fell on good soil. It came up and yielded a crop, a hundred times more than was sown."*

"This is the meaning of the parable: The seed is the word of God. Those along the path are the ones who hear, and then the devil comes and takes away the word from their hearts, so that they may not believe and be saved. Those on the rocky ground are the ones who receive the word with joy when they hear it, but they have no root. They believe for a while, but in the time of testing they fall away. The seed that fell among thorns stands for those who hear, but as they go on their way they are choked by life's worries, riches and pleasures, and they do not mature. But the seed on good soil stands for those with a noble and good heart, who hear the word, retain it, and by persevering produce a crop" (Luke 8:5-8,11-15).

Before truly believing and receiving Jesus, the soil of our lives is not good enough to grow the seed of our relationship with Him, and we can do nothing to clean it up. However, Jesus did that for us on the cross, and truly believing and receiving Him gives us a new life along with the new soil to allow our relationship with Him to grow.

WE ARE GOD'S MASTERPIECE
The apostle Paul describes our salvation experience at the Narrow Gate and it is worth reading with our hearts wide open.

But God is so rich in mercy, and he loved us so much, that even though we were dead because of our sins, he gave us life when he raised Christ from the dead. (It is only by God's grace that you have been saved!) For he raised us from the dead along with Christ and seated us with him in the heavenly realms because we are united with Christ Jesus. So God can point to us in all future ages as examples of the incredible wealth of his grace and kindness toward us, as shown in all he has done for us who are united with Christ

Jesus. God saved you by his grace when you believed. And you can't take credit for this; it is a gift from God. Salvation is not a reward for the good things we have done, so none of us can boast about it. For we are God's masterpiece. He has created us anew in Christ Jesus, so we can do the good things he planned for us long ago (Ephesians 2:4-10 NLT).

Created anew in Christ, we are the masterpieces of God. Although we know that we are not there yet, God sees us as who we will become as we travel the Narrow Road with Jesus as Lord of our lives. Paul offers this prayer for us as we begin our new lives in Christ. *When I think of all this, I fall to my knees and pray to the Father, the Creator of everything in heaven and on earth. I pray that from his glorious, unlimited resources he will empower you with inner strength through his Spirit. Then Christ will make his home in your hearts as you trust in him. Your roots will grow down into God's love and keep you strong. And may you have the power to understand, as all God's people should, how wide, how long, how high, and how deep his love is. May you experience the love of Christ, though it is too great to understand fully. Then you will be made complete with all the fullness of life and power that comes from God* (Ephesians 3:14-19 NLT).

IN THAT MOMENT

Perhaps your journey to this point took some time, thought and prayer; or it could be a decision that you are making without preparation, but with clear faith that your salvation is a gift from God.

You are experiencing Jesus' personal escort through the Narrow Gate as you commit your life to Him. You are asking forgiveness for all of your past life on the Broad Road and you believe that God provides that forgiveness to you as His gift. You believe that Jesus truly paid the wages and penalties for all of your sins in the past and those you will commit in the future. You trust that your sin record is erased and that you are reborn to be the person that God created you to be. Furthermore, you are being adopted into God's eternal family.

In addition to accepting Jesus as your Savior, you are submitting to Him as Lord of your life going forward – and that is a big surrender because you do not know exactly what that means and how your life will change. You are trusting that Jesus will help remove the strongholds of your life, but you are also submitting all other elements of your life to Him to manage. You are committing to trust the Lord with all your heart and refrain from leaning on your understanding. This is an all-in commitment to follow Jesus as both Savior and Lord of your life.

And with that decision and commitment, Jesus carries you through the Narrow Gate onto the Narrow Road to life. This is a personal moment between you and Jesus and the beginning of your relationship with Him.

DISCUSSION AND REFLECTION

1. 2 Corinthians 5:17 says we are reborn as new creations. Is that merely theology or does it translate into day-to-day life? If so, how?

2. Describe and discuss what takes place in that amazing moment of being carried through the Narrow Gate. Why is that the most significant moment of your life?

3. Why couldn't God simply forgive us and allow us to live on the Narrow Road for the remainder of our earthly lives? Discuss

righteousness and justice as it relates to God. Why do we have to be reborn as new creations?

4. Read Ephesians 2:4-10 and see how we begin to be God's masterpiece at the moment of our salvation.

Part 3 – A NEW LIFE

It is an understatement to say that life changes as we begin our new lives on the Narrow Road. We learned in 2 Corinthians 5:17 that we are reborn as new creations with the opportunity for a new life and purpose. The reality is that it takes some time to grow and mature into the people that God recreated us to be. Fortunately, the Bible provides us with a good preview of that journey.

What happens next and the speed at which it happens depends on our commitment and perseverance to allow Jesus to be the Lord of our lives. Because we do not know what that means, faith and trust are integral parts of our relationship with Christ. That is the way to begin our relationship with Jesus and the way to continue it as we take our last breath here on earth. *Trust in the Lord with all your heart and lean not on your own understanding; in all your ways submit to him, and he will make your paths straight* (Proverbs 3:5-6).

In his letter to the Ephesians (4:17-32), Paul describes some of the changes that take place over time as we trust in the Lord. Lies and deceptions are replaced with truth and integrity. Anger is controlled, with amends being made before the day is over. The desire to serve and give to others overrides selfish habits. Abusive language is

43

replaced by words of encouragement. Ongoing grudges and bitterness are replaced by forgiveness, reconciliation, and kindness. Then throughout the Bible, we learn how to truly become free of strongholds like pride, deception, feeling unloved, rejection, addiction, guilt, despair, unforgiveness, depression, sexual strongholds, and more. We learn that it takes our effort and commitment, but that we cannot possibly be changed without trusting the Lord and inviting the power of the Holy Spirit to overcome our old habits and influence of the enemy.

In Part 3, we look to God's Word to see how our lives change as we allow Jesus to be our Lord. *Don't copy the behavior and customs of this world, but let God transform you into a new person by changing the way you think. Then you will learn to know God's will for you, which is good and pleasing and perfect.* (Romans 12:2 NLT). Along this journey, we grow closer to God, find freedom, discover our God-given purpose, and begin making a difference. We begin to understand why this earthly life is the way it is and we learn how to best navigate through it. Life has purpose and significance, but we also discover that this new journey is not always easy.

A new life is what true believers have when they follow Jesus as their Lord. They have different talents and resources but share the commitment to glorify the Father and fulfill the commission of Jesus. If this is not your life today as a professed Christian, your next step is to draw close to God and allow Him to show you the way.

7. First-generation Disciples

L ooking at the lives of first-generation disciples is another way for us to see examples of people who have believed and received Jesus as the Lord of their life. God graciously provides enough information for us to see the servant-relationship these people had (and continue to have) with Him.

ROLE MODELS

We typically think of role models as people to be imitated – often beyond the reach of who we are or can be. However, the first generation of Jesus' disciples were real men and women who showed us that life in that role is often not easy. Carrying the gospel into the world generates opposition, and it is often difficult to know how to handle it.

Although traveling with Jesus initially sounds like a great opportunity, we might reconsider when we imagine the drama of what they experienced. If not for their utmost faith in Jesus, together with the supernatural support and power of the Holy Spirit, they might well have experienced what we know today as PTSD. Imagine the flashbacks, nightmares, and anxiety that could have consumed them as they experienced the life and death of Jesus. Add to that the threats and opposition they faced after Jesus ascended to heaven.

These first-generation disciples left whatever they had been doing to follow Jesus, believing that He was the promised Messiah. They felt called by God and must have been euphoric seeing the miracles that Jesus performed. They were likely amazed to hear the words and actions of Jesus that showed a new way of life that was still consistent with the Old Testament. They were following the future King, but would later be confused and disheartened when He would be inhumanely tortured and crucified to death. Even though Jesus told His disciples in advance of His fate, they didn't want to believe it would happen. Promising to come to His defense, Peter said, *"Never, Lord!" he said. "This shall never happen to you!"* (Matthew 16:22). How could He be the promised Messiah and not end up ruling the nation of God's chosen people? Their human minds and emotions called for a political and spiritual ruler, but God's plan was different than their expectations. Even before that traumatic event, Jesus' disciples faced choices about whether or not to continue to follow Him. *On hearing it, many of his disciples said, "This is a hard teaching. Who can accept it?" From this time many of his disciples turned back and no longer followed him. "You do not want to leave too, do you?" Jesus asked the Twelve. Simon Peter answered him, "Lord, to whom shall we go? You have the words of eternal life. We have come to believe and to know that you are the Holy One of God"* (John 6:60, 67-69). Some of His followers were selective in what they were willing to believe, but Jesus did not dilute His message of God's truth.

There was also the personal danger of being a follower of Jesus. His disciples dodged several conflicts throughout Jesus' ministry, but the physical threat became extreme as Jesus was arrested, tried, tortured, and crucified. They felt they were on the most wanted list and feared for their lives. As they went into hiding, imagine the conversations, flashbacks, and sleepless nights as they tried to sort out what would happen next. That had to be the low point of their three-year journey with Jesus, and as most of us do, they likely projected the downward trend to continue. Then three days later, they heard a report that Jesus had been seen alive. Before long, Jesus, in a resurrected body, appeared among them in their room behind locked doors! Imagine the roller-coaster ride of emotions from despair to unbelievable joy.

It was beginning to make sense. Jesus completed His mission as Savior, paying the wages of sin and providing the opportunity for all people to be forgiven, reborn, and accepted into God's eternal family. He rose from the dead and was back in their presence – hopefully, to establish His kingdom on earth. Expectations and hope must have again been high for most of those forty days He remained on earth. But God's plan was for Jesus to commission His disciples and then return to heaven. God's delegation of responsibility is worth noting because we are now the disciples with that commission. As such, we need to know what His plan is and accept our role in it. The bottom line is that all of us today have the same assignment and responsibility that Jesus gave to the first-generation disciples.

THE COMMISSION

The disciples didn't understand why Jesus wasn't staying to finish the job of establishing His earthly kingdom. They weren't ready for their role in God's plan, and they knew it. Their Lord was returning to heaven, the world around them was threatening, and they didn't know what to do next. Jesus replied to them with assurance, but they didn't quite understand how He was answering their prayer. *Then they gathered around him and asked him, "Lord, are you at this time going to restore the kingdom to Israel?" He said to them: "It is not for you to know the times or dates the Father has set by his own authority. But you will receive power when the Holy Spirit comes on you; and you will be my witnesses in Jerusalem, and in all Judea and Samaria, and to the ends of the earth"* (Acts 1:6-8).

Imagine being part of that small group and being tasked to continue and even extend Jesus' ministry to the ends of the earth. And, they were called to do that without Jesus in their presence. Jesus told them not to begin with their commission until they were baptized with the Holy Spirit. *"Do not leave Jerusalem but wait for the gift my Father promised, which you have heard me speak about. For John baptized with water, but in a few days you will be baptized with the Holy Spirit"* (Acts 1:4-5).

Although they had Jesus' promise of the Holy Spirit to help, they likely had no idea what that meant. Besides, they had a close relationship with Jesus and likely could not imagine how that could continue without Him in their presence. Fortunately, they found that Jesus' relationship with them did continue, as it does with us today as adopted children of God.

THE HOLY SPIRIT AT PENTECOST

Suddenly Jesus arose and was gone from sight with two men (angels) appearing to explain His future return. *"Men of Galilee,"* they said, *"why do you stand here looking into the sky? This same Jesus, who has been taken from you into heaven, will come back in the same way you have seen him go into heaven"* (Acts 1:11). As instructed, they went back and waited for the power of the Holy Spirit to commence their great commission. A few weeks later, when they were all together in a room, the Holy Spirit came upon them, and they were filled with His power and direction to make disciples.

Those same disciples who had been in fear to the point of hiding and denying they even knew Jesus, were suddenly fearless and convincing orators to crowds of unbelievers. Even more surprising was that many people in these crowds were believing and receiving Jesus. *When the people heard this, they were cut to the heart and said to Peter and the other apostles, "Brothers, what shall we do?" Peter replied, "Repent and be baptized, every one of you, in the name of Jesus Christ for the forgiveness of your sins. And you will receive the gift of the Holy Spirit. The promise is for you and your children and for all who are far off—for all whom the Lord our God will call"* (Acts 2:37-39). With the power of the Holy Spirit, these believers continued their commission from Jesus to make disciples.

APPLICATION TO US TODAY

God knew we would need information and examples of how we can be disciples. So, He arranged for nine people to write the New Testament consisting of four gospels plus twenty-three other books and letters. This New Testament provides God's plan for salvation and Jesus' commission for us as His disciples.

Now is the time for us to come together in Christ and live for the glory of God. Jesus created the opportunity for our eternal salvation, and He provides the road for our journey forward. Because the devil opposes us, we must know the truth and follow the direction of Jesus from the Holy Spirit. The Bible provides the unchanging foundation of truth, and the Holy Spirit communicates to us the counsel of Jesus for how to apply God's Word to our life. As we draw near to God as His adopted children, He promises to draw near to us with wonder that is beyond anything we can imagine.

DISCUSSION AND REFLECTION

1. Think about your role models now and in the past. Is it realistic to think that we should have role models from the Bible? Was the world too different then or is it much the same except for technology?

2. What are some things you have in common with the first-generation disciples? Consider not only the things they did right but also the struggles they faced and the mistakes they made.

3. Discuss Peter's reaction to jump in and protect Jesus as described in Matthew 16:22. Then consider Jesus immediate reply: *"Get behind me, Satan! You are a stumbling block to me; you do not have in mind the concerns of God, but merely human concerns"* (Matthew 16:23). How does that exchange relate to us today?

4. *Then Jesus said to his disciples, "Whoever wants to be my disciple must deny themselves and take up their cross and follow me. For whoever wants to save their life will lose it, but whoever loses their life for me will find it* (Matthew 16:24-25). Now think about that in terms of our subject verse of Matthew 7:21-23. Looks like there is no room for being a half-way committed Christian.

8. Grow and Mature Spiritually

New believers often have the motivation and excitement to tell the world of their Gift who is Jesus, but as spiritually immature children they are not yet ready for the opposition from the enemy.

The apostles and disciples who lived and traveled with Jesus had the opportunity to grow in their relationship with Him. They also learned the truth directly from the Lord and experienced how He handled the opposition. Although we do not have that same in-person opportunity, we do have all we need to communicate with Him as we navigate through life.

The apostle Paul is an excellent example for us because he did not come on the scene until after Jesus rose to heaven. Saul, his Hebrew name, was a Jew who knew about God from his extensive knowledge of the Old Testament Scripture. However, he did not recognize Jesus as the promised Messiah. Instead, he sided with the religious establishment seeing Jesus as a fraud and threat to their control.

Saul commanded respect and authority from the Jewish community as well as from the Roman empire because he also held Roman citizenship. Because he did not accept Jesus as the Savior, Saul directed the persecution and death of Christians with the intent of defending his Jewish faith. That continued until the Spirit of Jesus confronted Saul on the road to Damascus. *He fell to the ground and heard a voice say to him, "Saul, Saul, why do you persecute me?"* (Acts 9:4). Realizing he had missed the truth that Jesus was the long-awaited Messiah, Saul also understood that Jesus was confronting him with the gift of salvation. We know that Saul believed and received Jesus and was adopted into God's eternal family.

However, Saul was not yet ready to go into the world in his new life in Christ because he was a spiritual child. Saul knew God forgave him, but he still needed freedom from many strongholds of his life before. He also needed to know God's plan for his life ahead. Saul did not have the New Testament writings to find answers like we are blessed to have, but he did have the Holy Spirit living within him. So, Saul went into seclusion for three years, allowing God to feed his spiritual growth and maturity rather than immediately going back into the world. *I want you to know, brothers and sisters, that the gospel I preached is not of human origin. I did not receive it from any man, nor was I taught it; rather, I received it by revelation from Jesus Christ. For you have heard of my previous way of life in Judaism, how intensely I persecuted the church of God and tried to destroy it. I was advancing in Judaism beyond many of my own age among my people and was extremely zealous for the traditions of my fathers. But when God, who set me apart from my mother's womb and called me by his grace, was pleased to reveal his Son in me so that I might preach him among the Gentiles, my immediate response was not to consult any human being. I did not go up to Jerusalem to see those who were apostles before I was, but I went into Arabia. Later I returned to Damascus.* (Galatians 1:11-17).

When he got back into life with others, Saul knew his God-given purpose and his role in it. He had learned how to effectively communicate with the one true God and receive the power of the Holy Spirit as he went into the world to make disciples. Paul (his name to the Gentiles) was called to bring the message of Christ beyond the Jewish culture to the Gentile world – a calling that we thank God for giving to him. We also thank God for Paul's writings of the New Testament in which we see how to live as true believers on the Narrow Road to life.

THE VINE

Although it is humbling to know we begin our Narrow Road journey as spiritually immature children, it is comforting to be assured that Jesus is there to help us grow and mature. If we don't acknowledge our immaturity, we begin with excitement and great intentions, only to discover we are not the disciples Jesus wants us to be. It is easy to stall-out on the Narrow Road and conclude that God has nothing particular for us to do, as I know from experience. We cannot do this without God and we have to be actively engaged and committed. Jesus explains it this way: *"I am the vine; you are the branches. If you remain in me and I in you, you will bear much fruit; apart from me, you can do nothing* (John 15:5).

Just knowing that every true believer, regardless of physical age, must grow and mature provides us with a sense that our rebirth is a long-term gift. Rather than being impatient, we are called to enjoy the process of our spiritual growth and maturity. But the question remains, how do we grow, and what is our role in making it happen?

DISCUSSION AND REFLECTION

1. The need to grow and mature spiritually has a lot to do with the fact that we are reborn at the moment of our salvation. What

does that mean for someone who spent years attending church, maybe attending Bible studies, and spending time and money in service to help others? Describe your experience of growing or maturing – or your roadblocks in doing so.

2. New believers are often enthusiastic and eager to lead other people to know Jesus as both Savior and Lord. Can they be effective or should they have to wait until they grow spiritually and mature before going out into the world to make disciples? Since there is no limit to our spiritual growth, how do we know when to go forth and make disciples?

3. Discuss the approach taken by the apostle Paul following his encounter with the Spirit of Jesus on the road to Damascus. Relate that to our situation today for new believers who have jobs, families and ongoing commitments.

4. The fact that a branch is dependent on the vine for life is a good analogy for us to remember as we go forward on the Narrow Road to life. The question remains though, why do we not always turn to Jesus first in everything we think, say and do? What is our role in receiving the nourishment we need from Jesus as the vine?

9. Making It Happen

Without knowing more of God's plan, it is puzzling that our rebirth does not immediately make everything perfect and free from the chaos and evil of this world. However, as we grow to know God and mature spiritually with Jesus as Lord of our lives, we begin to see why life doesn't automatically become perfect at that moment. We also discover where God's plan is going, and we get a glimpse of the eternal perfection that awaits us. In the meantime, we need to know what God has planned for us in this new life and begin living it with Jesus as our Lord.

Although we are on the Narrow Road to life, we are surrounded by lost people who are living on the Broad Road to destruction, along with the enemy who continues to dominate this world. We are no longer subject to the enemy's influence, but his lies and deceptions can easily attract us unless we call on the resources that are provided by God. In that sense, we are on the defense, but we are also called by Jesus to be on the offense, leading lost people to discover the gift that we have received. Then if that is not enough of a challenge, we continue to have the day-to-day responsibilities we had before our salvation experience. We cannot make all of that happen on our own, yet we cannot sit back and expect God to change the world around us. This new life in Christ is a big challenge, but it is the way we grow to become the person God created us to be. We saw all of that in the Bible accounts of the first-generation disciples, and now we are the ones who must allow Jesus to direct our lives forward. Sure, we still have personal goals and dreams, but they must be placed on the table for the Lord to sort out and direct. We learn that nothing should be off-limits to the Lord as we grow closer to God. The theme of life forward must be, "I surrender all," allowing Jesus full control of who we are and what we do. This all-in commitment may initially be seen with fear, but for those of us who are trying to do that, there is no question that life with God is very good.

FAITH, COMMITMENT AND ACTION

So, making this new life in Christ happen requires our faith, commitment, and action. Initially, it seems that we don't have enough time to give to your commission. It may also seem difficult because we don't recognize God's communication with you. But He is likely saying, "draw close to me with all of your heart, and then I will be heard by you." Although we have a new spirit, we still have the same mind, old habits and thinking that need to be redirected to God.

My initial post-salvation efforts were like living in a foreign country with a language I did not know. The Bible was difficult for me to understand, and it was difficult to relate the situations and culture in the Bible to my life. I had to work at it before I began experiencing God's communication. It takes commitment to hear God. It is a process of doing life with Christ.

Fortunately, God provides enough direction to get us started and keep us going on our Narrow Road journey. Since we do not yet have the luxury of dining with Jesus to discuss what He has in mind for us to do tomorrow, we pray and turn to God's Word in the Bible.

With practice, that approach can work just as well, and we can look forward to dining with Him in the future. We will see a few ways to follow Jesus as His disciples, such as praying first, being the Church of true believers, making friends in Christ, finding freedom, and making a difference.

But even before discussing those tactical practices for our new lives, it helps to confirm God's purpose and see that each of us has a unique role in furthering that purpose. Then we will examine some of the ways that help us to grow into the people that He created us to be.

PURPOSE AND ROLE

We are called to give glory and honor to the one true God. *So whether you eat or drink or whatever you do, do it all for the glory of God* (1 Corinthians 10:31). With that in mind, Jesus assigns each of us to make disciples for the glory of God. This commission is intended to redirect our lives as the Apostle Paul so aptly illustrates. *But my life is worth nothing to me unless I use it for finishing the work assigned me by the Lord Jesus – the work of telling others the Good News about the wonderful grace of God* (Acts 20:24). As true believers, we do more than merely attend a Sunday church service, pray before meals, and turn to God in times of desperation. Instead, we intentionally allow God to develop a consuming desire in us for His purpose and for the roles that He created us to have in pursuing that purpose.

Before salvation, we were motivated by other purposes and often our situation defined our cause. But now, every person who truly believes and receives Jesus shares the same purpose – helping others to be disciples of Jesus. Also, because God graciously made each of us with different talents, skills, and personalities, we are called to take various roles in that common God-given purpose. We know from reading the New Testament that Jesus' disciples took on many roles, and it is clear that making disciples is a team effort. So, we need first to understand what it means to "make disciples" and then see some of the many roles that we can play in that team pursuit with Jesus as our Lord.

MAKING DISCIPLES

Making disciples can be seen from at least three perspectives. First of all, it means leading lost people to know Jesus as the one and only Savior and Lord. Like Paul, some people today are called to go into remote areas of the world to spread the gospel. Others are called to translate the Word of God into languages that these disciples can use to teach the lost people about the one true God. Some people raise and provide funds that support these disciple-makers, while others provide intercessory prayer for their work. We also know there are millions of lost people who live among us, so the rest of us are called to make disciples in our current situation. *But how can they call on him to save them unless they believe in him? And how can they believe in him if they have never heard about him? And how can they hear about him unless someone tells them? And how will anyone go and tell them without being sent? That is why the Scriptures say, "How beautiful are the feet of messengers who bring good news!"* (Romans 10:14-15 NLT).

A second facet of making disciples is to grow and mature as disciples of Jesus. That takes an intentional and ongoing effort on our part to know God, find freedom, and make a difference. Along with knowledge, we need the maturity that comes from trials, struggles, and successes with Jesus as the Lord of our lives. This part of making disciples is essentially allowing ourselves to be made into disciples. *Then we will no longer be infants, tossed back and forth by the waves, and blown here and there by every wind of teaching and by the cunning and craftiness of people in their deceitful scheming. Instead, speaking the truth in love, we will grow to become in every respect the mature body of him who is the head, that is, Christ. From him, the whole body, joined and held together by every supporting ligament, grows and builds itself up in love, as each part does its work.* (Ephesians 4:14-16).

And then, as we grow and mature, our commission includes helping other true believers to grow and mature spiritually. *And the things you have heard me say in the presence of many witnesses entrust to reliable people who will also be qualified to teach others* (2 Timothy 2:2).

The Great Commission is great, both because of its purpose and because of the magnitude of the effort involved. We cannot do it alone – we need other believers, we need the Lord to show us the way, and the Holy Spirit to provide the power to overcome all of the obstacles we will face.

PRAY FIRST

Prayer, in the name of Christ Jesus, is the foundation of a believer's relationship with God. Furthermore, the need for that prayer applies to every church body as well. Without that as the foundation, the church is without the Holy Spirit's presence and the living Word of God..

Of course, Jesus' prayerful relationship with the Father has always been in place, and He needed that for His mission here on earth. With success and without sin, Jesus navigated this sinful, chaotic, and corrupt earthly world for over thirty years as a man. And as a man, He could have been influenced by the world, but He was not. As a man, He depended on His relationship with the Father, and prayer was the way Jesus kept it active and alive.

As a human child and young adult, Jesus worked to translate His divine relationship with the Father into a human relationship that He would need for His ministry. *And the child grew and became strong; he was filled with wisdom, and the grace of God was on him* (Luke 2:40). Although we do not know all details of how that took place, we know He prayed fervently throughout His ministry's challenging years. He began His day in private prayer with the Father and continued that communication throughout each day. We often pray to get out of a situation that could have been avoided had we prayed first as Jesus did.

The apostles and first-generation disciples also provide us with examples of how prayer helps us to navigate through this challenging life. A few of those are:

Prayers of Request We are encouraged to take our requests to God, and He wants us to be committed to repeatedly asking for His help and acknowledging that we need Him for everything we do. *Do not be anxious about anything, but in every situation, by prayer and petition, with thanksgiving, present your requests to God* (Philippians 4:6). The key is that we request God's assistance in everything rather than only when in desperate situations.

Prayers of Thanksgiving Just as God wants our requests in everything we do, so does He want us to acknowledge our gratitude in the name of the Lord, Jesus. *And whatever you do, whether in word or deed, do it all in the name of the Lord Jesus, giving thanks to God the Father through him* (Colossians 3:17).

Prayers of Worship Jesus tells us to *worship the Father in the Spirit and in truth* (John 4:23-24). True worship is adoring God for who He reveals Himself to be, even if we do not fully understand the magnitude of His godliness. Worship is done through prayer as well as through other expressions of adoration such as music. Worship takes place in the church, but it also should take place in everything we do. He wants us to realize that everything good is through and from Him and that He is deserving of our unlimited and all-in worship. We spend incredible amounts of time, money, and emotion worshiping things and people of this world – all of which He deserves to receive. But we cannot sincerely worship God unless we know Him in truth as He reveals Himself to us in the Holy Bible. Only then will we begin to realize why He deserves our worship. *Sing to the Lord, all the earth; proclaim his salvation day after day. Declare his glory among the nations, his marvelous deeds among all peoples. For great is the Lord and most worthy of praise; he is to be feared above all gods. For all the gods of the nations are idols, but the Lord made the heavens. Splendor and majesty are before him: strength and joy are in his dwelling place* (1 Chronicles 16:23-27).

Prayers of Intercession As part of our new life in Christ, we find ourselves praying for lost people who cause problems for us and others. *But I tell you, love your enemies and pray for those who persecute you* (Matthew 5:44). We also pray for true believers who are our friends in Christ and members of God's eternal family.

Prayers of Spiritual Warfare As we know from the Word of God, the devil is our formidable and influential enemy in this earthly life. However, as newly adopted children in God's eternal family, we are encouraged to pray for God to overcome the enemy as we face the evil of this fallen world. Jesus understands what we are facing because He too repelled the enemy with the same divine resources that are available to us. Ephesians 6:10-12 says, *Finally, be strong* *in the Lord and in his mighty power. Put on the full armor of God, so that you can take your stand against the devil's schemes. For our struggle is not against flesh and blood, but against the rulers, against the authorities, against the powers of this dark world and against the spiritual forces of evil in the heavenly realms.* We draw on the power of God's Word as the sword of the Spirit and we pray in perseverance and holiness.

LORD, TEACH US TO PRAY

The apostles had been taught in the Jewish faith to pray, but after routinely watching Jesus go off in private to pray, they realized there must be something more to it. So Jesus taught them what we know as the Lord's Prayer as an example of speaking to God with adoration, consecration, petition, intercession, and protection. Furthermore, Jesus cautioned them not to pray to get recognition by others and not to babble on with words of meaningless repetition. *And when you pray, do not keep on babbling like pagans, for they think they will be heard because of their many words"* (Matthew 6:7).

Jesus also taught us to pray by example like on the night immediately before His suffering and crucifixion. This heartfelt prayer is recorded as the entire 17th chapter of the Gospel of John.

Jesus Prays To Be Glorified

After Jesus said this, he looked toward heaven and prayed: "Father, the hour has come. Glorify your Son, that your Son may glorify you. For you granted him authority over all people that he might give eternal life to all those you have given him. Now this is eternal life: that they know you, the only true God, and Jesus Christ, whom you have sent. I have brought you glory on earth by finishing the work you gave me to do. And now, Father, glorify me in your presence with the glory I had with you before the world began.

Jesus Prays For His Disciples

"I have revealed you to those whom you gave me out of the world. They were yours; you gave them to me and they have obeyed your word. Now they know that everything you have given me comes from you. For I gave them the words you gave me and they accepted them. They knew with certainty that I came from you, and they believed that you sent me. I pray for them. I am not praying for the world, but for those you have given me, for they are yours. All I have is yours, and all you have is mine. And glory has come to me through them. I will remain in the world no longer, but they are still in the world, and I am coming to you. Holy Father, protect them by the power of your name, the name you gave me, so that they may be one as we are one. While I was with them, I protected them and kept them safe by that name you gave me. None has been lost except the one doomed to destruction so that Scripture would be fulfilled.

"I am coming to you now, but I say these things while I am still in the world, so that they may have the full measure of my joy within them. I have given them your word and the world has hated them, for they are not of the world any more than I am of the world. My prayer is not that you take them out of the world but that you protect them from the evil one. They are not of the world, even as I am not of it. Sanctify them by the truth; your word is truth. As you sent me into the world, I have sent them into the world. For them, I sanctify myself, that they too may be truly sanctified.

Jesus Prays For Us Today

"My prayer is not for them alone. I pray also for those who will

believe in me through their message, that all of them may be one, Father, just as you are in me and I am in you. May they also be in us so that the world may believe that you have sent me. I have given them the glory that you gave me, that they may be one as we are one— I in them and you in me—so that they may be brought to complete unity. Then the world will know that you sent me and have loved them even as you have loved me.

"Father, I want those you have given me to be with me where I am and to see my glory, the glory you have given me because you loved me before the creation of the world.

"Righteous Father, though the world does not know you, I know you, and they know that you have sent me. I have made you known to them, and will continue to make you known in order that the love you have for me may be in them and that I myself may be in them."

BE THE CHURCH

We need the Church, but the Church is not what many people assume it to be. It is not a building, not a religion, and not a nonprofit organization. Instead, the Christian Church is the collection of true believers of the one true God. All people who have truly believed and received Jesus are the Church. *"Just as there are many parts to our bodies, so it is with Christ's body. We are all parts of it, and it takes every one of us to make it complete, for we each have different work to do. So we belong to each other, and each needs all the others"* (Romans 12:4-5 TLB).

The Church is described as the body of Christ, and each of us is a unique part with a specific God-given purpose. *The human body has many parts, but the many parts make up one whole body. So it is with the body of Christ. Some of us are Jews, some are Gentiles, some are slaves, and some are free. But we have all been baptized into one body by one Spirit, and we all share the same Spirit. If one part suffers, all the parts suffer with it, and if one part is honored, all the parts are glad* (1 Corinthians 12:12-13; 26 NLT).

We are the Christian Church, and our purpose together is to glorify the one true God as we pursue Jesus' commission to make disciples. We routinely gather together to praise and worship God and to be reminded and refreshed on what this life is about according to Him. We do that in church and with small groups of friends in Christ.

FRIENDS IN CHRIST

The Acts of the Apostles and other books of the New Testament are filled with stories of how the first-generation disciples worked together. The apostle Paul wrote to his friends in Rome with these words: *I long to see you so that I may impart to you some spiritual gift to make you strong— that is, that you and I may be mutually encouraged by each other's faith* (Romans 1:11-12). They shared the common God-given purpose of giving honor and glory to God and making disciples of Jesus, but they also had the same day-to-day needs and struggles that we have today. They depended on each other to live with the challenges and joys of life. The world of lost people offers a variety of associations and assumed friendships, but true Christians need friends in Christ. As fellow disciples in Christ, we help each other to grow spiritually and face the enemy as we navigate through this challenging life on the Narrow Road.

The first generation of disciples gathered in small groups as Jesus encouraged them to do: *"For where two or three gather in my name, there am I with them"* (Matthew 18:20). The writer of Hebrews tells us: *And let us consider how we may spur one another on toward love and good deeds, not giving up meeting together, as some are in the habit of doing, but encouraging one another* (Hebrews 10:24-25). Paul tells us that our small groups of fellow disciples can help us be accountable and encourage us to turn away from the evil attractions of the world: *Brothers and sisters, if someone is caught in a sin, you who live by the Spirit should restore that person gently. But watch yourselves, or you also may be tempted. Carry each other's burdens, and in this way, you will fulfill the law of Christ* (Galatians 6:1-2).

We need friends in Christ to grow in our relationship with Him. These are the people who share the same purpose and Narrow Road journey with us. We need each other because we are better together.

FIND FREEDOM

It is for freedom that Christ has set us free. Stand firm, then, and do not let yourselves be burdened again by a yoke of slavery (Galatians 5:1). When we truly believe and receive Jesus, we are set free from the penalty of our sins. However, we still have to be released from the strongholds of our previous lives before Christ. It is for freedom from those strongholds that Christ has set us free. Bitterness, rejection, fear, self-ambition, revenge, guilt, hate, insults, anger, pride, impurity, sadness, unforgiveness, abuse, betrayal, humiliation, persecution, blame, defeat, loss, shame, and failure are some of the strongholds that carry over to our new lives in Christ.

But Jesus provides us the opportunity for true freedom from these burdens. As we turn to His Word in the Bible and open our hearts to the Holy Spirit, we find His answer for every issue that interferes with our freedom to be the people He created us to be. As we trust Him as our Lord and allow the Holy Spirit to show us the way, the strongholds of the enemy are replaced by the freedom that is in Christ. *But whenever someone turns to the Lord, the veil is taken away. For the Lord is the Spirit, and wherever the Spirit of the Lord is, there is freedom. So, all of us who have had that veil removed can see and reflect the glory of the Lord. And the Lord—who is the Spirit—makes us more and more like him as we are changed into his glorious image* (2 Corinthians 3:16-18 NLT).

MAKE A DIFFERENCE

Most of us want to make a difference by helping others because we were created in the image of God. People throughout the world help others in small ways and grand ways as well. However, in light of eternal life with the one true God, we have to ask what it means to make a difference. The fact is that people who have not received Christ are doing many good works. But that means nothing to God in terms of their salvation. *For it is by grace you have been saved, through faith—and this is not from yourselves, it is the gift of God— not by works, so that no one can boast* (Ephesians 2:8-9).

Good works, when done by us who truly believe, can have immeasurable value to both the receiver and giver. The Bible goes on to say in verse 10: *For we are God's handiwork, created in Christ Jesus to do good works, which God prepared in advance for us to do.* In the name of Christ Jesus, we help other people, both fellow believers as well as people who are lost. When we do good works for fellow believers, we are helping them grow closer to God. When we do works for others, we should include the opportunity for them to know Jesus and grow closer to Him. That is how we make a difference. As we turn to Jesus as our Lord and listen to His direction through the Holy Spirit, we are shown many ways to give glory to God.

And finally, knowing that we are making a difference is often a matter of faith because we do not always get feedback on the impact we are having on the lives of others. But as we grow closer to God and follow the Lord, we have all of the joy and satisfaction we need to do more. We know in our hearts that we are God's masterpiece and we are doing the good works that He prepared us in advance to do.

A GROWING RELATIONSHIP

Our adoption as children of God is the beginning of our relationship with Him. From that point, we work to grow and mature as we go forward in life with Jesus as Lord and with the Holy Spirit living within us. We pray first and turn to God's Word as truth to defend against the enemy's spiritual warfare. Our relationship with God grows as we do life with Him.

DISCUSSION AND REFLECTION

1. Although good works are not in any way related to our gift of salvation, they are expected after our saving relationship with Jesus is established. Discuss this new expectation and why true believers of Christ do not view works and service as an obligation.

2. How are our efforts to grow and mature spiritually dependent on our relationship with Jesus?

3. Discuss the promise that God will carve us into the unique masterpiece that He created each of us to be? How does that affect your attitude and approach to daily life?

4. What are some of your current priorities, goals, and dreams that need to be submitted to God to prioritize and possibly dismiss according to His will? If you are not doing this, are you saying that you can manage these efforts better than God?

5. Are you open to a new priority such as Jesus' commission to make disciples? Is your life already so busy that you cannot

imagine how you can give enough attention to this? Even if you have the time, are there other reasons you are not acting on this commission?

6. Discuss some roles God might have for you as part of Jesus' commission to make disciples.

7. We know that effective communication is an essential part of any relationship. With God, prayer is communication. Discuss how prayer is now part of your life and what improvements could be made. When and how are you going to make that happen?

8. Is the church you attend filled with the Holy Spirit and unconditionally aligned with the Word of God in the Bible? If so, get involved and be the church. If not, pray for that to happen or find one that is.

9. Do you have a core group of friends who are true Christians and followers of Christ Jesus? If you are associated with a Spirit-filled church, those people are there and are welcoming people like you to give glory to God and follow Jesus as Lord of your life.

10. Discuss some of the strongholds that can (but don't have to) influence the lives of true believers after we believe and receive Jesus as Savior and Lord. Do you believe that God has the power to eliminate every one of those strongholds? Do you know how to find His answers? What is your next step to receive the freedom that you need?

Part 4 – KNOW GOD AND HIS PLAN

The next six chapters allow you to see if you are believing in the one true God, or some god of assumptions and lies from the enemy. It is so easy to assume that God is someone He is not. The lies and deceptions of the enemy can have us worshiping a false god without knowing. How can we expect to be a disciple of Jesus if we do not know the truth of who He is? How can we turn to the powerful resource of the Holy Spirit if we do not know how He lives within us? Fortunately, God provides the way to know the truth of God and His plan.

People typically have many acquaintances, but we only have a few best friends and personal relationships that grow throughout the years. The one true God wants to be the very best of our best friends here on earth as He will be in heaven. That relationship begins at the moment of our salvation when we receive Jesus as our Savior and grows from that point forward. At least that is what God hopes will happen. On the other hand, the enemy works to keep our relationship with God from growing. As the father of lies, Satan tries to convince us that God is someone He is not, so we will not draw close to Him. The enemy also tries to convince us that God has lost control of this earthly life and has abandoned any plan He may have had.

The truth is that God does reveal Himself to those of us who want to know Him and are willing to participate in building a relationship with Him. Not only does He allow us to know Him, but He also shares His plan for this earthly life and beyond. With that knowledge, life makes much more sense and we see hope in the present and future. *If people can't see what God is doing, they stumble all over themselves; but when they attend to what he reveals, they are most blessed* (Proverbs 29:18 MSG).

10. The One True God

Without knowing, most people believe in a god who is not. In other words, because people do not know the truth of what God reveals in the Bible and through the Holy Spirit, they assume God to be someone other than who He is. Those assumptions originate from the lies and deceptions of the enemy and become the prevailing worldview of people who have not been adopted as children of God. As a result, most people (including many professed Christians) are worshiping false gods and building their lives upon assumptions and lies rather than upon the absolute truth of God.

Scholars have combed the Bible to identify the characteristics of God, but those descriptors merely allow us to know about Him. Reading a description of someone as fun and loving does not come close to communicating the actual joy and love that people share. Many of God's attributes relate to what we know, but others are beyond anything that we have yet experienced:

God is infinite, self-existing, and without beginning and end. *Before the mountains were born or you brought forth the whole world, from everlasting to everlasting you are God* (Psalm 90:2).

God is immutable, meaning His nature and attributes never change, providing us with assurance in all of His promises. *"I the Lord do* *not change...* " (Malachi 3:6).

God is self-sufficient and has no needs. *"I make known the end from the beginning, from ancient times, what is still to come. I say, 'My purpose will stand, and I will do all that I please.' From the east I summon a bird of prey; from a far-off land, a man to fulfill my purpose. What I have said, that I will bring about; what I have planned, that I will do* (Isaiah 46:10-11).

God is omnipotent or all-powerful, assuring us that His plan for life is on track and will be completed despite the opposition from the enemy. *"I know that you can do all things; no purpose of yours can be thwarted"* (Job 42:2).

God is omniscient, which means he knows everything – past, present, and future. *Great is our Lord and mighty in power; his understanding has no limit* (Psalm 147:5).

God is omnipresent meaning he is always everywhere, allowing us to know that we are never alone. *The eyes of the Lord are everywhere, keeping watch on the wicked and the good* (Proverbs 15:3).

God is wise with perfect wisdom. *"To God belong wisdom and power; counsel and understanding are his* (Job 12:13).

God is faithful and true, keeping His promises. *"Know therefore that the LORD your God is God; he is the faithful God, keeping his covenant of love to a thousand generations of those who love him and keep his commands"* (Deuteronomy 7:9).

God is good. *O, taste and see that the Lord is good"* (Psalm 34:8). We experience that goodness in all situations when we acknowledge Him in all we do.

God is just. *He is the Rock, his works are perfect, and all his ways are just. A faithful God who does no wrong, upright and just is he* (Deuteronomy 32:4).

God is merciful, compassionate, and kind. *All the paths of the Lord are mercy and truth, to such as keep His covenant and His testimonies* (Psalm 25:10 NKJV).

God is gracious, providing both common grace and saving grace that we neither deserve nor can earn. *The LORD is gracious and compassionate, slow to anger and rich in love* (Psalm 145:8).

God is love, well beyond our understanding of the word. *Your love, Lord, reaches to the heavens, your faithfulness to the skies. Your righteousness is like the highest mountains, your justice like the great deep* (Psalm 36:5-6).

God is holy, meaning set apart and perfect in all of His attributes. *"There is no one holy like the Lord; there is no one besides you; there is no Rock like our God* (1 Samuel 2:2).

God is three persons of Father, Son, and Holy Spirit, yet He is one God. *Then God said, "Let us make mankind in our image, in our likeness..."* (Genesis 1:26). *"Therefore, go and make disciples of all nations, baptizing them in the name of the Father and of the Son and of the Holy Spirit..."* (Matthew 28:19). All persons of God have these same attributes as each is the same God.

THE LIVING WORD

Another way to discover the nature of God is from His revelations as we prayerfully read the Bible. It is called the Living Word because the words come alive and relate to each believer.

At first, our readings often generate more questions than answers.

However, as we become more acquainted with the Word of God and with God Himself, we are led to His answers. Of course, at some point, we understand that Jesus is the answer to all questions. *For all of God's promises have been fulfilled in Christ with a resounding "Yes!" And through Christ, our "Amen" (which means "Yes") ascends to God for his glory* (2 Corinthians 1:20 NLT). However, understanding God's Word is not always easy, and at times we are appalled at God's answers and actions. They may not conform to our preconceived notions of who God is and we push back or ignore what we read. Some religious leaders even promote changing the Word of God because their definitions make more sense and will attract more people to believe in God. But God is who the Bible says He is, and Jesus confirmed that by not compromising His words and actions to attract more followers.

When our loyalty to the world is replaced with our submission to Jesus as Savior and Lord, He reveals Himself in ways that allow us to know more of who He is. When that happens, we go from merely knowing about Him to having a growing relationship with Him. At the same time, God reminds us that we cannot possibly comprehend all that He is: *"For my thoughts are not your thoughts, neither are your ways my ways," declares the LORD. "As the heavens are higher than the earth, so are my ways higher than your ways and my thoughts than your thoughts* (Isaiah 55:8-9).

APPROACH

Knowing the truth about God helps our relationship with Him to grow. We pray for our heart to be open for the revelations of the Holy Spirit as we turn to the Bible to learn about God,

The approach we take to know God is clear: *Come close to God, and God will come close to you. Wash your hands, you sinners; purify your hearts, for your loyalty is divided between God and the world* (James 4:8 NLT).

We also grow closer to God as we examine His actions and words in the context of His plan for life. From that perspective, we are in a better position to understand why this earthly life is the way it is today and how it will be in the future.

GOD'S PLAN FOR LIFE

As we watch the evening news, it is tempting to turn to God and ask, "What are you thinking? Is this what you intend for this earthly life?" God would likely say that He has described His plan for life, and we have not bothered to learn what that is. *Thomas said to him, "Lord, we don't know where you are going, so how can we know the way?"* (John 14:5). But we do know where God is going, and we do know the way when we open our hearts to read the Word of God and receive the power of the Holy Spirit to relate His Word to our lives.

Sure, we know that Adam and Eve sinned, but why did God's plan not account for that? Or did it? We also know of many other events in both the Old and New Testament eras, but how do they all fit into God's plan? And what about the traumatic happenings like the 9/11 attack and similar events around the world? Are these parts of His plan, or are they happening because His plan isn't working? And then, if God's plan does explain all of what is now going on, does it also have answers for how we can best navigate through it?

Details of God's plan and answers to those questions are revealed throughout the Bible. We know that because God provides prophecies that are later confirmed. His plan is firm and has always been there. And now we can see the prophecies that remain as His plan nears a conclusion.

Many professed Christians understand the big picture of God's plan, but not as many know the details of what happened, why it happened, and how the past events continue to impact our lives today. An old German proverb, "Der liebe Gott steckt im detail", translates as God is in the detail. A more recent version is "The devil is in the details," and the Bible explains how both statements are true. We will see much more of what God reveals about His plan and Himself.

DISCUSSION AND REFLECTION

1. If we assume God to be someone other than who He is, our relationship is with someone other than God. Discuss examples of deceptions, lies, and misinformation about God that Satan is successfully using to keep us from knowing Him.

2. Discuss some of the many attributes of God as described in the Scripture. Are there any of His characteristics you find difficult to accept or understand?

3. Do you see this quest to know the truth about God as part of a Bible study, or rather as a foundation for your daily life going forward?

4. Why do we need to know the truth about God to do what Paul says in 2 Corinthians 13:5? *"Examine yourselves to see whether you are in faith; test yourselves…"*

5. We know that Adam and Eve sinned, but why did God's plan not account for that? Or did it? And what about the traumatic happenings like the 9/11 attack and similar events around the world? Are these parts of His plan, or are they happening because His plan isn't working?

11. In the Beginning

Knowing the truth of what happened in the beginning, allows us to make sense of life and know God better. Without this truth, we naturally make assumptions to help us explain and cope with this life.

Most people look to experts in science, philosophy, psychology, media, and social media for answers. However, their advice is often based often on theories and assumptions, rather than the truth of God's Word. So, why do we go to these "experts" when we have the Word of God as truth? God answers that question as well.

BEFORE THE BEGINNING WAS GOD

Before creation, God existed. Everything we see had a beginning, but God did not. The Bible tells us: *"In the beginning, God created the heavens and the earth."* Obviously, God existed before the beginning to do that. The one true God has always existed and always will. *"I am the Alpha and the Omega,"* says the Lord God, *"who is, and who was, and who is to come, the Almighty"* (Revelation 1:8). Psalm 90:2 tells us: *Before the mountains were born or you brought forth the whole world, from everlasting to everlasting you are God.*

Because people throughout the world have so many different and conflicting understandings and beliefs about God, it is most important to know as much as He reveals to us about who He truly is. The one true God has always existed with a triune nature. While it is difficult for us to comprehend, the truth is that God is three persons – the Father, the Son, and the Holy Spirit. Genesis 1:26 introduces us to this fact: *Then God said, "Let us make mankind in our image, in our likeness."* Throughout the Bible, we learn how God employs His triune nature. The Son of God is described in Colossians 1:16-17: *For in him all things were created: things in heaven and on earth, visible and invisible, whether thrones or powers or rulers or authorities; all things have been created through him and for him. He is before all things, and in him all things hold together.* Then the Holy Spirit is referenced in Genesis 1:2: *Now the earth was formless and empty, darkness was over the surface of the deep, and the Spirit of God was hovering over the waters.*

Although this information about God may seem like more theology than we need to know, it is useful as we continue to discover God's plan for life and the many ways He provides for us to navigate through it.

PURPOSE OF THIS EARTHLY LIFE

This earthly life is the opportunity for each of us to choose whether we wish to live for eternity, giving God glory and honor. Since every person will live forever beyond the time of our present earthly bodies, God provides this brief period on earth as the time to choose, once and for all, how and where we will be living forever. *Yet to all who did receive him, to those who believed in his name, he gave the right to become children of God* (John 1:12).

TIME

It is also useful for us to see how time factors into our understanding of creation. Before creation, there was no point from which to base time since only God existed. As such, creation was also the beginning of time. Furthermore, God's creation of a daily sun-cycle provides us with a systematic way to measure time from that point forward. The reason to bring this into the conversation is that many people are being convinced to discount God's account of creation because it is described to have taken place in six days followed by one day of rest. *By the seventh day God had finished the work he had been doing; so on the seventh day he rested from all his work* (Genesis 2:2). While that sounds like an impossible task in any timeframe, He is God, and we are only beginning to comprehend what that means. Also, the Apostle Peter reminds us: *But do not forget this one thing, dear friends: With the Lord, a day is like a thousand years, and a thousand years are like a day* (2 Peter 3:8). An Old Testament Prayer of Moses says: *A thousand years in your sight are like a day that has just gone by, or like a watch in the night* (Psalm 90:4). Clearly, God understands time in ways that we do not. As such, it matters not that all of creation, including His day of rest, was completed in one hundred and sixty-eight hours of sixty minutes each. Furthermore, it matters not that each of those first seven days may not have been the same duration. What does matter is that all of creation was perfect in the beginning.

So, the earth can be billions of years old, but man can be relatively young. Looking at creation in this way, according to the Word of God, allows us to filter the deceptions of the enemy and see the truth about God's incredible creation.

GOD'S REASON FOR EVERYTHING

God tells us that everything is created for His glory. Furthermore, all of God's answers to our prayers are for that same purpose - His glory. *"I am the Lord; that is my name! I will not yield my glory to another or my praise to idols* (Isaiah 42:8). *So whether you eat or drink or whatever you do, do it all for the glory of God* (1 Corinthians 10:31). *"I will harden the hearts of the Egyptians so that they will go in after them. And I will gain glory through Pharaoh and all his army, through his chariots and his horsemen"* (Exodus 14:7).

At first, it is easy to see God's expectation for all glory as being selfish and contrary to what a loving God would want. We naturally feel that life is about us and our happiness, so that is what we strive to attain. But when we live for God's glory rather than our own, we discover that we receive the benefits of living according to His will and plan for life.

Another attribute of the one true God is that He explains Himself as being jealous. *"You must worship no other gods, for the LORD, whose very name is Jealous, is a God who is jealous about his relationship with you"* (Exodus 34:14 NLT). How can God proudly name Himself as Jealous? That may sound appalling until we see that God is jealous because of His love for us. When we live in any way other than for His glory, and according to His will, we hurt ourselves and others. And that He does not want for His adopted children.

Not to us, Lord, not to us but to your name be the glory, because of your love and faithfulness (Psalm 115:1).

CREATION OF THE HEAVENS AND HEAVENLY HOSTS

Some of us assume that the six creation-days involved only the earth and everything in and on it, but God also created the heavens and heavenly hosts during that period. *In the beginning, God created the heavens and the earth* (Genesis 1:1). *You alone are the LORD. You made the heavens, even the highest heavens, and all their starry host, the earth and all that is on it, the seas and all that is in them. You give life to everything, and the multitudes of heaven worship you* (Nehemiah 9:6). The heavens and heavenly hosts too were included in God's assessment on the sixth day as being *very good* (Genesis 1:31).

CREATION OF THE EARTH AND MAN

The earth was initially created as *formless and empty, darkness was over the surface of the deep, and the Spirit of God was hovering over the waters* (Genesis 1:2). Light was then introduced to the darkness, and day and night were created. The sky was separated from the water, and the water was separated from the land. Plants, vegetation, trees, and seed-bearing fruit were created, as were fish for the waters and birds for the skies. Days were organized into seasons and years. On day five, every sort of animal was created and each produced offspring of the same kind. Then on day six, human beings were created in the image of God. *Then God said, "Let us make human beings in our image, to be like us* (v. 26). *So God created human beings in his own image* (v. 27). *Then God blessed them and said, "Be fruitful and multiply. Fill the earth and govern it. Reign over the fish in the sea, the birds in the sky, and all the animals that scurry along the ground"* (v. 28). Finally, at the end of day six, God declared all of His creation to be *"very good"* (v. 31). *Thus, the heavens and the earth were completed in all their vast array* (Genesis 2:1).

A VERY GOOD CREATION

After God created everything and everyone, He declared his creation to be *"very good,"* then God rested on the seventh day. *On the seventh day God had finished his work of creation, so he rested from all his work. And God blessed the seventh day and declared it holy because it was the day when he rested from all his work of creation* (Genesis 2:2-3). Life began in that very good state and could have continued that way to this day and beyond. The first two people experienced the bliss of living God's way and were aware of how that life could have continued. They had perfect relationships with God, with each other and with the earth they were entrusted to manage. God provided everything the first two people needed as they lived together with Him. They were created in the image of God, and life was very good.

ANGELS AND DEMONS

Remember that God also created the heavens and heavenly hosts, and a once-perfect angel saw his perfection as equal to or greater than his Creator. Seeking the honor and glory that belongs to God alone, other angels joined with him, and a battle ensued. But Satan and his demons lost the battle and were cast down to earth. *You were anointed as a guardian cherub, for so I ordained you. You were on the holy mount of God; you walked among the fiery stones. You were blameless in your ways from the day you were created till wickedness was found in you. Through your widespread trade, you were filled with violence, and you sinned. So I drove you in disgrace from the mount of God, and I expelled you, guardian cherub, from among the fiery stones. Your heart became proud on account of your beauty, and you corrupted your wisdom because of your splendor. So I threw you to the earth; I made a spectacle of you before kings* (Ezekiel 28:14-17).

Later, Jesus said, *"I saw Satan fall like lightning from heaven"* (Luke 10:18), and Satan is seen as *"a star that had fallen from the sky to the earth"* (Revelation 9:1). Satan, meaning adversary, was cast to earth along with his legion of demons which numbered around one-third of the heavenly hosts (Hebrews 12:22). That is God's account of the very first sin and His response to it. At that point, life on earth was still perfect. However, the test for man was set as part of God's plan and Satan was in place to introduce the deception and lie that would change everything.

MAN AND SATAN

The first people knew nothing about Satan, but clearly understood they were not to eat from the Tree of the Knowledge of Good and Evil. They had everything needed to live comfortably without fruit from that forbidden tree. But they were curious, and with help from Satan, they reasoned that eating the fruit from the forbidden tree would allow them to know what God was hiding from them. If they ate from it, they would know everything about good and evil. They already knew about good because God used *"very good"* to describe His perfect creation they were enjoying. Evil was not understood except that it related to God's promise that they would die if they ate from that tree. Adam and Eve likely dismissed that threat because if God knew about both topics, then it would also be good for them to know. The Bible doesn't describe what they were thinking, but many of us would allow our thoughts to go along that line. Maybe God was implying that they would become more like Him if they ate from the Tree of the Knowledge of Good and Evil.

Then comes the false promise from Satan who appeared to be another friendly part of God's magnificent creation. They had no reason to suspect deception because they were living in a paradise without the dangers and threats we know today. However, God made His expectations clear, so there was no reason for them to entertain other suggestions.

Since he is a spiritual being, Satan entered the body of a harmless serpent to speak to Eve who was admiring the Tree of the Knowledge of Good and Evil. He couldn't force her to eat from that tree, but he could make a convincing argument to do so, even though it was a lie. *"You will not certainly die," the serpent said to the woman. "For God knows that when you eat from it your eyes will be opened, and you will be like God, knowing good and evil"* (Genesis 3:4-5).

They didn't bother to question what evil was, and they didn't ask God for clarification of what it would mean for their eyes to be opened and be like God. They knew they would be risking death, but since this was their first challenge to God, maybe they would get by with a warning. Besides, they may have thought, what is death anyway? We don't know if that was their thinking, but it is close to the way we think when faced with attractive temptations. At that moment, the attraction surpassed the risk, so they went for it.

In hindsight, we might wonder why God allowed Satan to enter the picture in the first place, and why he was allowed to attract the first people away from God with lies and deceptions. Of course, God knew the outcome in advance, so why would He allow his perfect creation to be destroyed? That answer comes into focus as we draw closer to God and begin to understand His plan for this earthly life journey. We know that we still have to deal with the lies and deceptions of Satan, but as true believers, we have the God-given power to do it.

A TEST

The fact is that God's plan for this earthly life includes tests of our commitment to provide honor and glory to Him. We may not like it, but this life is a test. And like Adam and Eve, we must choose between the will of the sovereign God and all other options. God made it simple to remember the choice. The Tree of Life was the spectacular reminder of the opportunity to glorify God and continue living His way. The other choice was the Tree of the Knowledge of Good and Evil that God told them to avoid under penalty of death. *The LORD God took the man and put him in the Garden of Eden to work it and take care of it. And the LORD God commanded the man, "You are free to eat from any tree in the garden; but you must not eat from the tree of the knowledge of good and evil, for when you eat from it you will certainly die"* (Genesis 2:15-17). Although they did not know the implications of death at that point, God made it clear they were not to go there, and that was all they needed to know.

Had man created a perfect universe, our focus may have been to install safeguards to keep it that way, but God has a different approach. Rather than make it impossible for anything or anyone to destroy His work, God does the opposite. God gives us the ability to choose and allows Satan to attract us away from Him. God intends this earthly life to be a defining test of our unconditional commitment to Him. And, He was willing to sacrifice both His perfect creation and His Son to allow us another opportunity to choose Christ Jesus and the Tree of Life for eternal life with Him.

LIFE WAS NO LONGER VERY GOOD

Of course, both Eve and Adam chose to follow Satan's advice to know evil as well as good. Immediately they felt shame in the presence of each other and God. Adam blamed Eve and Eve blamed the devil for the deception, but God never considered their excuses. God's response to their sin was immediate and profound. Satan was admonished: *And I will put enmity between you and the woman, and between your offspring and hers; he will crush your head, and you will strike his heel"* (Genesis 3:15). And while that did nothing to deter the devil from his resolve to separate man from God, this statement was the first prophecy of God's plan to send Jesus as the Messiah.

Man's pain and suffering were also previewed, as was the destruction of the earth. *To the woman, he said, "I will make your pains in childbearing very severe; with painful labor, you will give birth to children. Your desire will be for your husband, and he will rule over you." To Adam, he said, "Because you listened to your wife and ate fruit from the tree about which I commanded you, 'You must not eat from it, "Cursed is the ground because of you; through painful toil, you will eat food from it all the days of your life. It will produce thorns and thistles for you, and you will eat the plants of the field. By the sweat of your brow, you will eat your food until you return to the* ground *since from it you were taken; for dust you are and to dust, you will return"* (Genesis 3:16-19).

The life-giving relationship between God and man was severed. *And the Lord God said, "The man has now become like one of us, knowing good and evil. He must not be allowed to reach out his hand and take also from the tree of life and eat, and live forever." So the Lord God banished him from the Garden of Eden to work the ground from which he had been taken. After he drove the man out, he placed on the east side of the Garden of Eden cherubim and a flaming sword flashing back and forth to guard the way to the tree of life* (Genesis 3:22-24).

God foreknew the death and destruction that would result. The earth and even the heavens would degrade as we see today, and billions of people would reject God in favor of the attractions and lies of Satan. Although life appears as chaos to most people, it is understandable when we turn to the Word of God. We also learn that the best is yet to come for people who choose the one true God.

DISCUSSION AND REFLECTION

1. Knowing what took place in the beginning, has much to do with understanding why life is the way it is. Discuss why is it worthwhile to understand the details of how God's "very good" creation has gotten to be the way it is today.

2. Discuss the fact that this earthly life is a test for all of us to choose whether we wish to live God's way or our way for eternity. Furthermore, how do you feel about God allowing Satan to deceive the first people (and us) as part of that test?

3. Why is it that, even after we make the all-in commitment to believe and receive Jesus, we continue to be tested in other ways?

12. God the Father

The question exists even if we do not direct it to God: "Why did you not take into account that Adam and Eve were deceived by Satan? Then you could have coached them to learn the lesson, forgiven them, and allowed them to restart life." The answer is that God could not do that because of who He is. Because He is both good and just, He requires absolute goodness and justice. *He is the Rock, his works are perfect, and all his ways are just. A faithful God who does no wrong, upright, and just is he.* (Deuteronomy 32:4) God does not change who He is to conform to any situation. By siding with Satan to challenge the sovereignty of God, the very nature of man changed from being very good to being sinful. God's forgiveness alone would not recreate man's nature that had been destroyed. Furthermore, man could not do enough to undo or to recreate himself back to his original sinless nature. *Therefore, just as sin entered the world through one man, and death through sin, and in this way death came to all people because all sinned* (Romans 5:12).

While it appears to be an unsolvable problem, God's plan included the solution that only He could provide without compromising who He is. The opportunity for man to be reborn to his original state required justice to be served, at a price that only God could pay.

God knew what He had to do, and He did it. In the perfect timing of His plan, the Father sent His Son to pay the price and provide the opportunity for our salvation. However, that part of God's plan was far in the future. In the meantime, Adam and Eve and their descendants lived in a world of both good and evil. And having a sinful nature, along with Satan to influence their choices, the results were chaos, destruction, and death. Nevertheless, the Old Testament writings provide us with examples of a few people who chose to listen and relate to God. They were not perfect people by any measurement, but the Bible's accounts of their struggles and victories allow us to learn about the nature and characteristics of God. We can also see how God works with people who are living in a fallen world as we do today.

WELCOME TO EVIL

As described in Genesis 5, Adam and Eve populated the earth with children who grew and multiplied. Although man had shunned God and embraced evil, the loving God continued to be available to help those individuals who would listen. But most did not. Cain, a son of Adam and Eve, is an example. God heard Cain's frustration and counseled him, but he refused God and murdered his brother.

Evil manifests itself in many ways as we know very well today. Galatians 5:19-21 lists a few examples: *sexual immorality, impurity, and debauchery; idolatry and witchcraft; hatred, discord, jealousy, fits of rage, selfish ambition, dissensions, factions, and envy; drunkenness, orgies, and the like.* Although it is written throughout the Bible that God is patient and slow to anger, He does have limits as described in Genesis 6:5-7. *The Lord saw how great the wickedness of the human race had become on the earth, and that every inclination of the thoughts of the human heart was only evil all the time. The Lord regretted that he had made human beings on the earth, and his heart was deeply troubled. So the Lord said, "I will wipe from the face of the earth the human race I have created— and with them the animals, the birds and the creatures that move along the ground—for I regret that I have made them."*

However, God's love and His plan for life continued as He selected Noah and his family to survive the great flood. Noah was described in verse 8 as *a righteous man, blameless among the people of his time, and he walked faithfully with God.* After the flood, God made this covenant promise: *"Never again will I curse the ground because of humans, even though every inclination of the human heart is evil from childhood. And never again will I destroy all living creatures, as I have done* (Genesis 8:21). God made that promise knowing that every inclination of the human heart is evil and knowing that the sinful nature of man would again dominate life on earth.

A CHOSEN PEOPLE

Without reading the entire Bible, it is easy to conclude that God was showing favoritism by selecting one group of people for a particular role. After the flood, humanity had multiplied and spread throughout the land, and most people were again living without God. However, from the very beginning, God's plan included a promise to send a Messiah who would provide the opportunity for redemption from the sinful mess they had created for themselves. Because the Messiah would be born into our humanity, God's plan included the formation of one group of people to be the heritage nation for Him. *For you are a people holy to the Lord your God. Out of all the peoples on the face of the earth, the Lord has chosen you to be his treasured possession* (Deuteronomy 14:2). It is also important to note that the word "holy" means to set apart, rather than be perfect and sinless because that was not possible. So, as the first step of His plan for redemption, God chose a nation of people as an example of how to live with God in a sinful world. Israel would also become the heritage nation into which Jesus would be born as the Messiah.

For this reason, it is worthwhile for us to go to the Old Testament to learn how God worked with this chosen nation, and learn how people from that nation are models for us today. They are models, both in how to live, as well as in how not to live.

THE PATRIARCHS

God declared that the nation of Israel would descend from Abram who would later be renamed, Abraham. *The Lord had said to Abram, "Go from your country, your people and your father's household to the land I will show you. "I will make you into a great nation, and I will bless you; I will make your name great, and you will be a blessing. I will bless those who bless you, and whoever curses you I will curse, and all peoples on earth will be blessed through you"* (Genesis 12:1-3). *"I will establish my covenant as an everlasting covenant between me and you and your descendants after you for the generations to come, to be your God and the God of your descendants after you* (Genesis 17:7). Why God chose Abraham for this role was later revealed: *Clearly, God's promise to give the whole earth to Abraham and his descendants was based not on his obedience to God's law, but on a right relationship with God that comes by faith. If God's promise is only for those who obey the law, then faith is not necessary and the promise is pointless* (Romans 4:13-14 NLT).

So began God's redemption process, but it didn't happen quite as smoothly as we might imagine. Abram was already seventy-five years old at the time and had no children as descendants. By faith, he followed God's direction for the next two decades but he became increasingly concerned about his age and ability to have children.

However, God assured him: *"Look up at the sky and count the stars—if indeed you can count them." Then he said to him, "So shall your offspring be." Abram believed the Lord, and he credited it to him as righteousness* (Genesis 15:5). That was a promise of God, meaning it would happen regardless of the impossibility of Abram and Sarah to conceive and deliver a child at their ages. God's promise also included the prophecy that Abram's descendants would occupy the Promised Land.

Sarah then introduced her spin into God's plan as she became impatient. Thinking she could no longer bear a child, she told Abram to father a child with her maidservant Hagar. As a result, Ishmael was born and one of his descendants, Muhammad, would later establish the religion of Islam. However, another son, Isaac, was born directly to Sarah and Abraham. Isaac would continue God's plan as the father of God's chosen people, while Ishmael became the father of the Arab people. The enmity between Jews and Arabs to this day is a consequence of the impatience of Sarah and Abraham with God's promise.

After Hagar and Ishmael were sent away, God severely tested Abraham. *He said to him, "Abraham!" "Here I am," he replied. Then God said, "Take your son, your only son, whom you love—Isaac—and go to the region of Moriah. Sacrifice him there as a burnt offering on a mountain I will show you"* (Genesis 22:1-2). It is at times like these when we must remember that God's ways are far greater than our ways, teaching us the all-in commitment we need to have for His glory. That trial was not easy, but Abraham and Isaac grew closer to God with their faith and trust. Of course, that situation also provides us with a preview of the future event when God the Father would be sacrificing His Son for our Salvation.

Isaac continued the patriarchal role by marrying Rebekah and fathering Esau and Jacob. As the firstborn of twins, Esau should have received the traditional inheritance blessing, but Rebekah and Jacob interfered causing Jacob to go forward as the patriarch. Even when God's chosen people did not follow His will, His plan continued. Then God wrestled with Jacob causing him to know that He was in charge (Genesis 32:24-30). In that struggle, Jacob was renamed as Israel, the nation-name of God's chosen people.

THE NATION OF ISRAEL

Jacob had twelve sons who later became fathers of the twelve tribes of Israel. Because he was the favored son of Jacob, Joseph was overwhelmed by his brothers and sold to the Ishmaelites (descendants of Ishmael) as a slave. Jacob was told that wild animals had killed his son, but Joseph ended up alive in Egypt as a slave. He was later sent to jail for a crime he did not commit, but Joseph never lost faith in God. Then in a series of events that only God could orchestrate, Joseph was eventually elevated by Egypt's Pharaoh to second-in-command over all of Egypt. That journey was beyond anything anyone could imagine, and it all happened with Joseph's incredible faith in God.

MOSES

With Joseph's blessing, his brothers were forgiven and the people of Israel were given land in Egypt. They prospered for many years in communion with the people of Egypt, but that eventually changed when new Egyptian leadership saw the growing number of Hebrews as a threat. They were forced into slavery, and then the Pharaoh ordered midwives to kill all baby boys born to Hebrew girls. However, God's selection of the baby Moses for a future role in His plan allowed him to escape the death sentence. Ironically, Moses was rescued from the Nile River by the daughter of the Egyptian Pharaoh and raised as a son. Again, we learn that God's ways are far beyond anything we can imagine, and He often selects ordinary people like Moses to carry out His plan.

At age forty, Moses fled Egypt, and later from the burning bush, he was called by God to go back to lead God's chosen people to the Promised Land. *But Moses said to God, "Who am I that I should go to Pharaoh and bring the Israelites out of Egypt?" And God said, "I will be with you. And this will be the sign to you that it is I who have sent you: When you have brought the people out of Egypt, you will worship God on this mountain"* (Exodus 3:11-12). Moses was reluctant because he was a wanted man in Egypt, and also because he wasn't sure the Hebrew people would want to follow him. *God said to Moses, "I am who I am. This is what you are to say to the Israelites: 'I am has sent me to you.'" God also said to Moses, "Say to the Israelites, 'The Lord, the God of your fathers—the God of Abraham, the God of Isaac and the God of Jacob—has sent me to you.' "This is my name forever, the name you shall call me from generation to generation* (Verse 14-15).

God also gave Moses a preview of what he would face and assured him: *But I know that the king of Egypt will not let you go unless a mighty hand compels him. So I will stretch out my hand and strike the Egyptians with all the wonders that I will perform among them. After that, he will let you go. "And I will make the Egyptians favorably disposed toward this people so that when you leave you will not go empty-handed* (v. 19-21). But even with God speaking directly to him through the burning bush and assuring him of what he would face, Moses was still reluctant as we might be. *Moses said to the Lord, "Pardon your servant, Lord. I have never been eloquent, neither in the past nor since you have spoken to your servant. I am slow of speech and tongue." The Lord said to him, "Who gave human beings their mouths? Who makes them deaf or mute? Who gives them sight or makes them blind? Is it not I, the Lord? Now go; I will help you speak and will teach you what to say." But Moses said, "Pardon your servant, Lord. Please send someone else"* (Exodus 4:10-13).

This exchange allows us to know more about God and know we can speak to Him as a wise and loving Father. Reading this in context, we see that God listened to Moses and allowed his brother Aaron to go along as Moses' spokesman. God's plan continued without compromise while He still listened to Moses and answered his prayer.

THE PASSOVER

The meetings of Moses and Aaron with the Pharaoh were not going well. Pharaoh's heart continued to harden, as God said it would, and the Hebrew people suffered the consequences as the plagues were rolled out. They could not understand why Moses was causing more problems for them. Moses and Aaron were caught in the middle between God's will and the consequences that were plaguing the very people God was professing to be helping. *Moses returned to the Lord and said, "Why, Lord, why have you brought trouble on this people? Is this why you sent me? Ever since I went to Pharaoh to speak in your name, he has brought trouble on this people, and you have not rescued your people at all"* (Exodus 4:22-23). What an example for us who cannot understand why God allows things to happen.

God knew well in advance how all of this would play out. *The Lord said to Moses, "When you return to Egypt, see that you perform before Pharaoh all the wonders I have given you the power to do.*

But I will harden his heart so that he will not let the people go. Then say to Pharaoh, 'This is what the Lord says: Israel is my firstborn son, and I told you, "Let my son go, so he may worship me." But you refused to let him go; so I will kill your firstborn son'" (Exodus 4:21-23).

That final plague, known as the Passover, broke Pharaoh's resolve to hold the Hebrews in captivity and that event has much significance to us today. God told the Israelites, "*Then they shall take some of the blood* (from each sacrificial lamb) *and put it on the two doorposts and the lintel of the houses in which they eat it. For I will pass through the land of Egypt that night, and I will strike all the firstborn in the land of Egypt, both man and beast; and on all the gods of Egypt I will execute judgments: I am the Lord. The blood shall be a sign for you, on the houses where you are. And when I see the blood, I will pass over you, and no plague will befall you to destroy you, when I strike the land of Egypt"* (Exodus 12:7,12-13 ESV).

Why would God do that? Every firstborn Egyptian child was killed, but all of His chosen people were spared as long as they followed God's command to sprinkle the blood of a sacrificial lamb on the doorpost of their homes. God's plan for this earthly life-journey is far beyond anything we can assume. Imagine the chaos of that situation as Pharaoh surrendered to the God of Moses and Aaron. *Pharaoh and all his officials and all the Egyptians got up during the night, and there was loud wailing in Egypt, for there was not a house without someone dead. During the night Pharaoh summoned Moses and Aaron and said, "Up! Leave my people, you and the Israelites! Go, worship the Lord as you have requested. Take your flocks and herds, as you have said, and go. And also bless me"* (Exodus 12: 30-32). Although it wasn't clear at that time, this Passover event was a preview of the future sacrifice of Jesus, as the spotless Lamb, to atone for the sins of those who would choose to believe and receive the one true God.

WANDERING IN THE DESERT

The departure of the Israelites from Egypt was smooth, and the Egyptians gave them supplies and riches for their journey to the land promised by God for their nation. But soon they began to question Moses (and God) because they no longer had the comforts they had as slaves in Egypt. At the same time, Pharaoh realized that Egypt desperately needed the Israelites as slaves, so he sent his troops to overcome them. Of course, we know that God intervened to part the Red Sea and destroy the Egyptians in pursuit. *Moses answered the people, "Do not be afraid. Stand firm and you will see the deliverance the Lord will bring you today. The Egyptians you see today you will never see again. The Lord will fight for you; you need only to be still"* (Exodus 14:13-14).

They began that journey without trusting God, and adverse results quickly showed. Nevertheless, God provided for all their needs and offered help for them to know His will. At times they did give glory and honor to God, but often they did not. At times they did follow His commandments, but often they did not. Because of their lack of trust in God, they wandered the desert for forty years before being allowed by God to enter the Promised Land. The distance from Egypt of 250 miles could have been traveled in eleven or twelve days.

THE PROMISED LAND

Because Moses temporarily broke faith with God and, as leader of the Israelites, did not uphold His holiness, he was permitted only to see the Promised Land from a distance before he died. Joshua became the leader taking the Israelites into Canaan, the land that was promised to them as a nation. However, even then, their struggles continued. They still needed to defeat the Canaanites for the land, and they needed to follow God's way to do it. Initially, they did, but soon returned to their sinful ways and failed to win possession of the entire promised land. Not until two hundred years later under Kings David and Solomon did Israel gain control of the whole land that had been promised by God. But then they lost portions of that land as they continued to violate their covenant relationship with God.

JUDGES

Although the Israelites considered themselves to be one nation, the twelve tribes lived in different areas of the Promised Land and no longer had one leader, like Moses or Joshua, to communicate God's message. The tribes fought among themselves, and God provided judges to lead them back to Him. People repented and turned back to God for a time, but then returned to their sinful ways. The Book of Judges provides lessons and examples of people who answered God's call amid dramatic and violent struggles. God disciplined the Israelites for following other gods and disregarding their covenant relationship. Nevertheless, He never abandoned His chosen people and used those chaotic times to advance His plan. Judges provided direction, but only the Israelites' full commitment to God would get them back on track.

KINGS

The Israelites wanted a king like other countries telling Samuel: *"You are old, and your sons do not follow your ways; now appoint a king to lead us, such as all the other nations have"* (1 Samuel 8:5). Samuel was disturbed and prayed to God for direction. God was also disturbed, telling Samuel that His plan was for the Israelites to look to Him as their King. *And the Lord told him: "Listen to all that the people are saying to you; it is not you they have rejected, but they have rejected me as their king. As they have done from the day I brought them up out of Egypt until this day, forsaking me and serving other gods, so they are doing to you. Now listen to them; but warn them solemnly and let them know what the king who will reign over them will claim as his rights"* (1 Samuel 8:7-9).

Samuel repeated God's message and warned of the consequences of having a king other than God. *But the people refused to listen to Samuel. "No!" they said. "We want a king over us. Then we will be like all the other nations, with a king to lead us and to go out before us and fight our battles"* (1 Samuel 8:19-20).

Although God did not condone their appointment of a king, He did advise them to minimize the influence of a godless king. *"When you enter the land the Lord your God is giving you and have taken possession of it and settled in it, and you say, 'Let us set a king over us like all the nations around us,' be sure to appoint over you a king the Lord your God chooses"* (Deuteronomy 17:14-15).

Kings ruled the Israelite nation for the next 464 years until the Babylonians overran it in 586 BC. During that time the Israelites split into two kingdoms of Judah and Israel and eventually were ruled by several kings and one queen. Of the forty-two rulers, only twelve began their reign with the intent of allowing God to rule through them and only five of those completed their reign that way. With that godless leadership, it is easy to see why the nation of God's chosen people went astray. God knew this would happen as He told Samuel before the first king was appointed: *When that day comes, you will cry out for relief from the king you have chosen, but the Lord will not answer you in that day"* (1 Samuel 8:18). God's plan was for Israel to follow Him as their King, but they refused, and ultimately, their nation paid the price.

PROPHETS

Prophets were another way that God communicated with people of the Old Testament. The word prophet comes from two Greek words, "pro" which means before and "fayme" which means to speak. The Apostle Peter tells us how prophecy relates to God: *"No prophecy of Scripture came about by the prophet's own interpretation of things. For prophecy never had its origin in the human will, but prophets, though human, spoke from God as they were carried along by the Holy Spirit"* (2 Peter 1:20-21).

The prophets and prophecies given by God are important parts of God's plan. Because so many of the prophecies have already been proven true, we know that all of God's Word can be accepted as truth. Furthermore, although all prophesies have not yet been fulfilled, all that have are true.

Prophesies also help us to know God, know His will, and know His plan. Prophecies about Jesus' life and death as our Messiah have all been validated, and God's prophesies of end times and eternal life assure us that this earthly life is merely a brief journey to eternal life. These prophecies continue to be an essential communication from God to us.

CONCLUSION OF THE OLD TESTAMENT ERA

As the Old Testament era approached the final seven hundred or so years, the Jewish nation struggled to keep itself together, which is not surprising given its inconsistent record of honoring God. During this period, the Jewish people were ruled by several nations, including the Assyrians, Babylonians, Greeks, Egyptians, and

Romans. The Jerusalem temple, built four hundred years earlier by King Solomon, was destroyed when the Babylonians captured the city. Seventy years later, when captivity by the Babylonians ended, a revival among the Jews took place, and the temple and city of Jerusalem were rebuilt. These dramatic events are more than history because they reinforce our knowledge of God. He is faithful to His people, He judges and administers justice for sin, and He is absolute with His promises, and covenants.

During the final four hundred years of the Old Testament era, God did not speak to the Jewish people. However, there was no doubt that His communication would resume as the book of Malachi points forward to the coming of the Messiah: *"I will send my messenger, who will prepare the way before me. Then suddenly the Lord you are seeking will come to his temple; the messenger of the covenant, whom you desire, will come,"* says the Lord Almighty (Malachi 3:1). Prepare and wait for the Messiah is the concluding message from God for the next period. He didn't say when, but He did promise a messenger (John the Baptist) who would announce Jesus as the Messiah.

OLD TESTAMENT SUMMARY

There was no beginning for the one true God who has always existed and always will. However, at one point, He created all that we know of today and more. God created the heavens, the earth, the heavenly spirits, and all living things on earth, and He did all of that for His glory. God created human beings in His image, and this earthly time of life to choose whether or not we want to glorify Him for eternity. Adam and Eve chose to challenge the sovereignty of God in favor of knowing evil as well as good. The nature of man immediately changed from righteous to sinful and was then inherited by all of us as their descendants. Man could not possibly reverse the damage done. While that appeared to be a hopeless situation, God made an early promise that He would, at some point, pay the price for man to be reborn as a new creation. In the meantime, God's love for His creations continued throughout the Old Testament era. Because God is love, He continued to coach people and provide all of their needs. But the lies and deceptions of the enemy continued to be more attractive for most people who kept moving away from God. Knowing that most people would never listen, God's plan included a chosen group of people to be the example of how life could best be lived in this sin-filled world. The relationship between God and the Hebrew people provides the foundation for us today to know God and to know the struggles of navigating through this earthly life.

However, even if His chosen people had done everything God told them to do, His plan required a New Testament era with specific actions that only God could take. For any person to again have the opportunity to live as part of the eternal family of God, the wages of sin had to be paid, and only God could do that at an extreme cost. *For the wages of sin is death, but the gift of God is eternal life in Christ Jesus our Lord* (Romans 6:23).

In the final book of the Old Testament, God tells us the next step of His plan is for the Messiah to arrive and do what no man could do.

DISCUSSION AND REFLECTION

1. This Old Testament summary is used here to highlight a few situations that allow us to know more about God the Father. Describe some things you learned about God that you did not previously know – even though you may have been familiar with the situation.

2. What are some things you learned about God that you find

disturbing or hard to believe? If you dismiss these, how can your relationship with God grow? How can you get to the point where these attributes of God are no longer disturbing?

3. Assumed Christians often focus on the New Testament in their quest to come closer to God and that is often enough to be led through the Narrow Gate of Salvation. Why is it worthwhile to also be familiar with the Old Testament?

4. At some point, consider reading the Bible from cover to cover. You will likely do that more than once because of your desire to know God and hear Him speak to you. As a start, consider reading the Old Testament with the specific purpose of knowing the personality and qualities of God the Father.

13. The Messiah

Now as we turn to know the Son of God, we get the added benefit of learning more about God the Father because as Jesus said, *"If you really know me, you will know my Father as well"* (John 14:7). Inviting Jesus to be our Lord and lead us forward in life requires us to know Him personally. It also requires our intentional effort because of the demands, attractions, and deceptions of this world. At the same time, Jesus wants us to know Him as Lord and actively helps to make it happen.

Four hundred years had passed since the last prophesies of the Old Testament, and the Jewish people continued to exist as a nationality of people but not as a sovereign nation. The Jews were subject to the Roman Empire but were still allowed to have Herod the Great as their leader. Herod was successful in keeping the Romans happy and preserving his rule. However, he was viewed by the Jews as a cruel and brutal tyrant who would crush all opposition. When Herod heard that the future king of the Jews had been born, his immediate response was to make sure that Jesus was killed. *When Herod realized that he had been outwitted by the Magi, he was furious, and he gave orders to kill all the boys in Bethlehem and its vicinity who were two years old and under, in accordance with the time he had learned from the Magi* (Matthew 2:16). Keep in mind that Herod was killing the children of his nation. He cared not for the salvation of his people, but instead for the preservation of his power. It is also amazing to realize that this action by Herod was also the fulfillment of a prophecy of God through Jeremiah six hundred years before. *This is what the LORD says: "A voice is heard in Ramah, mourning and great weeping, Rachel weeping for her children and refusing to be comforted, because they are no more"* (Jeremiah 31:15).

Of course, Jesus survived that threat and grew as a child and young adult. His earthly father was a craftsman and Jesus grew up in a family setting. As part of a traditional Jewish household, Jesus also studied Scripture as part of His education. At the same time, his parents knew He was the Son of God, so it must have been an interesting family life. At age twelve on a family trip to Jerusalem, Jesus showed He was no ordinary pre-teen. *After three days they found him in the temple courts, sitting among the teachers, listening to them and asking them questions. Everyone who heard him was amazed at his understanding and his answers. When his parents saw him, they were astonished* (Luke 2:46-48).

As part of God's plan, four thousand years had elapsed from the time God created the first people until Jesus was born onto this earth. Jesus was and still is the only resolution to the problem that man created when choosing to know evil as well as good. As God, Jesus became a man to solve the problem that man is incapable of solving. Understanding more about Jesus can help us appreciate the sacrifice that God made for our eternal salvation.

THE NATURES OF CHRIST

We have already established that the one true God is three persons in the Father, Son, and Holy Spirit. Now we learn that God's plan is for His Son, as God, to become man and make it possible for sinful people to be reborn as righteous new creations.

The supernatural birth of Jesus allowed Him to be both fully God and man. *The angel went to her and said, "Greetings, you who are highly favored! The Lord is with you"* (Luke 1:28). *And the angel answered her, "The Holy Spirit will come upon you, and the power of the Most High will overshadow you; therefore the child to be born will be called holy—the Son of God* (Luke 1:35 ESV). Shortly after that and before they came together, an angel of the Lord spoke to Joseph who was engaged to Mary saying: *"Joseph son of David, do not be afraid to take Mary home as your wife, because what is conceived in her is from the Holy Spirit. She will give birth to a son, and you are to give him the name Jesus because he will save his people from their sins"* (Matthew 1:20-21). That was the means God used to send His Son into the world, allowing Him to have both the nature of God and the nature of man without sin. This supernatural birth fulfilled the promise that God made in Genesis 3:15 immediately after the fall of man.

During Jesus' ministry, no one questioned His humanity. He was born like other babies and grew as a child, into adulthood. He became hungry, thirsty, tired, and physically weak as all other people do. Before the resurrection, Jesus' body was like ours in every respect. After the resurrection, His body was glorified, as ours will be when Jesus returns, and we are raised from the dead.

Jesus also had a human mind that learned how to talk, read, write, and grow in maturity and wisdom. *Then he went down to Nazareth with them and was obedient to them. But his mother treasured all these things in her heart. And Jesus grew in wisdom and stature, and in favor with God and man* (Luke 2:51-52).

We can relate to Jesus because of His humanity, and He certainly can relate to us. However, Jesus remained sinless: *For we do not have a high priest who is unable to empathize with our weaknesses, but we have one who has been tempted in every way, just as we are— yet he did not sin* (Hebrews 4:15).

It is also useful to know that Jesus did not rely on His divine nature to resist temptation as we learn from His experience in the wilderness immediately following His baptism. As preparation for His ministry, the Holy Spirit led Jesus to fast and be alone for forty days in desolate conditions. That preparation included experiencing temptation as a human in need. *Then Jesus was led by the Spirit into the wilderness to be tempted by the devil. After fasting forty days and forty nights, he was hungry. The tempter came to him and said, "If you are the Son of God, tell these stones to become bread"* (Matthew 4:1-3). Rather than using his divine powers, *Jesus answered, "It is written: 'Man shall not live on bread alone, but on every word that comes from the mouth of God'"* (Matthew 4:4).

For this reason, he had to be made like them, fully human in every way, in order that he might become a merciful and faithful high priest in service to God, and that he might make atonement for the sins of the people. Because he himself suffered when he was tempted, he is able to help those who are being tempted (Hebrews 2:17-18).

JESUS' LIFE ON EARTH

The four gospels and the first part of Acts of the Apostles describe Jesus' life on earth. Each gospel provides a variety of details, but all are consistent in describing who Jesus is and what He did. Two of the gospels also trace Jesus' ancestry back to the Old Testament, showing Him to be the promised Messiah. Jesus' mission as Savior was to personally pay the wages of sin for all who receive Him. His mission as Lord was, and still is, to be the example of how His disciples should live God's way – even in this fallen world dominated by Satan and lost people. Following is a summary of significant events in the life of Jesus.

JESUS' MINISTRY BEGINS

Jesus kept a low profile for the first thirty years, then suddenly He was on the scene being welcomed by John the Baptist, God the Father and the Holy Spirit. *In those days John the Baptist came, preaching in the wilderness of Judea and saying, "Repent, for the kingdom of heaven has come near." This is he who was spoken of through the prophet Isaiah: "A voice of one calling in the wilderness, 'Prepare the way for the Lord, make straight paths for him'"* (Matthew 3:1-3).

John had many followers but he proclaimed that he was not the Messiah: *"I baptize you with water for repentance. But after me comes one who is more powerful than I, whose sandals I am not worthy to carry. He will baptize you with the Holy Spirit and fire* (Matthew 3:11). *Then Jesus came from Galilee to the Jordan to be baptized by John. But John tried to deter him, saying, "I need to be baptized by you, and do you come to me?" Jesus replied, "Let it be so now; it is proper for us to do this to fulfill all righteousness." Then John consented. As soon as Jesus was baptized, he went up out of the water. At that moment, heaven was opened, and he saw the Spirit of God descending like a dove and alighting on him. And a voice from heaven said, "This is my Son, whom I love; with him, I am well pleased"* (Matthew 3:13-17). The Spirit then led Jesus to prepare for His ministry, going into the wilderness for forty days of fasting, prayer, and temptation by Satan.

After that, Jesus came back on the scene to begin His ministry as the Messiah. He had no followers and nothing to promote His ministry except the grace and power of God along with His commitment to do the will of the Father. In a brief three-year period, Jesus would not only provide the opportunity for eternal salvation, but He would also introduce the next stage of God's plan showing us how to live and what to do as adopted children of God.

He was educated, articulate, and knew Scripture, but the leaders and establishment of the Jewish religion did not want anyone on the scene who might be challenging their control and power.

THE BAPTISM OF JESUS

Jesus' baptism allowed Him to identify with the sinners whose sins He would soon bear on the cross. *God made him who had no sin to be sin for us, so that in him we might become the righteousness of God* (2 Corinthians 5:21). This act of water baptism symbolized His death (submersion) and resurrection (coming up from the water) as the long-awaited Messiah of lost people. His ministry had begun.

JESUS CALLS HIS DISCIPLES

They didn't know Him yet, but they had faith enough to leave their lives to follow Him. *As Jesus was walking beside the Sea of Galilee, he saw two brothers, Simon called Peter and his brother Andrew. They were casting a net into the lake, for they were fishermen. "Come, follow me," Jesus said, "and I will send you out to fish for people." At once, they left their nets and followed him* (Matthew 4:18-20). Ten other men were called and followed Jesus as His apostles. They were not prominent people and had no qualifications for the work they would be doing. Jesus calls all of us, but few respond for many different reasons. Fortunately for some of us who are reluctant to answer, He typically calls more than once and in different ways.

MIRACLES

Jesus performed miracles so that others might believe that He is the Son of God. He changed water into wine, walked on water, calmed the wind, healed the sick, raised a man from the dead, fed thousands of people and more. These were simple illustrations that God is much greater than we are and His solutions to our problems are often beyond our imagination. His miracles also provided a spotlight on the truth of His teaching. *Jesus performed many other signs in the presence of his disciples, which are not recorded in this book. But these are written that you may believe that Jesus is the Messiah, the Son of God, and that by believing you may have life in his name* (John 20:30-31).

SERMON ON THE MOUNT

Many followers of Jesus had gathered on what was likely a pleasant weather day. When Jesus saw the crowds, he went up on the mountainside and sat down to speak to His followers. There is no indication it was a planned event, but the content of Jesus' sermon was most significant. At least nineteen topics were succinctly covered, leaving no room for misinterpretation. Jesus also dismissed legalism and works-based salvation while still confirming His adherence to the law. *"Do not think that I have come to abolish the Law or the Prophets; I have not come to abolish them but to fulfill them* (Matthew 5:17).

This sermon was the occasion when Jesus warned us about being assumed Christians, telling us that He needs to know us as people who truly believe and receive Him. *"Not everyone who says to me, 'Lord, Lord,' will enter the kingdom of heaven, but the one who does the will of my Father who is in heaven. On that day many will say to me, 'Lord, Lord, did we not prophesy in your name, and cast out*

demons in your name, and do many mighty works in your name?'
And then will I declare to them, 'I never knew you; depart from me,
you workers of lawlessness'" (Matthew 7:21-23 ESV). Jesus also
confirmed that warning with His road trip analogy: *"Enter through*
the narrow gate. For wide is the gate and broad is the road that
leads to destruction, and many enter through it. But small is the gate
and narrow the road that leads to life, and only a few find it
(Matthew 7:13-14).

THE TRANSFIGURATION

The Transfiguration was a special occasion that Jesus shared with
only three of His close friends and apostles, Peter, James, and John.
Although they had been traveling with and closely watching Jesus
for some time, these men knew Jesus as a man. They believed He
was the Son of God, but they could not imagine the greatness of His
divinity. About a week after Jesus told his disciples that He would
suffer, be killed, and later raised to life, He took them up a mountain
to pray. *There he was transfigured before them. His face shone like*
the sun, and his clothes became as white as the light. Just then there
appeared before them Moses and Elijah, talking with Jesus
(Matthew 17:2-3). As we might expect, Peter began speaking about
the situation when God the Father interrupted. *While he was still*
speaking, a bright cloud covered them, and a voice from the cloud
said, "This is my Son, whom I love; with him I am well pleased.
Listen to him!" When the disciples heard this, they fell facedown to
the ground, terrified. But Jesus came and touched them. "Get up,"
he said. "Don't be afraid." When they looked up, they saw no one
except Jesus (v. 5-8). Suddenly they had a better perspective on the
fact that Jesus was truly the Son of God.

PALM SUNDAY

Most Jews believed the Messiah would come to rule as an earthly king restoring and preserving their sovereign nation, and they expected this was the moment He would appear as their king-to-be. A huge crowd lined the road with coats and palm branches giving Jesus the royal treatment as He rode into the city on a donkey and fulfilling the prophecy of Zechariah some five hundred years earlier (Zechariah 9:9). They wanted a political Messiah rather than a spiritual one, and to that expectation, Jesus was a big disappointment. It was the week of Passover, and before that event the Jews would turn against Jesus and insist that the Romans crucify Him and remove Him from their lives. Of course, we know that Jesus would go on to complete his mission of salvation for everyone who truly believes He is the way, the truth, and the life eternal (John 14:6).

THE LAST SUPPER

Knowing the suffering that He was about to face, Jesus still used His last meal time with his apostles as a teaching moment. They observed the Passover meal, and Jesus related it to His suffering and death for our salvation. *While they were eating, Jesus took bread, and when he had given thanks, he broke it and gave it to his disciples, saying, "Take and eat; this is my body." Then he took a cup, and when he had given thanks, he gave it to them, saying, "Drink from it, all of you. This is my blood of the covenant, which is poured out for many for the forgiveness of sins. I tell you, I will not drink from this fruit of the vine from now on until that day when I drink it new with you in my Father's kingdom" (Matthew 26:26-29).*

Jesus also used that occasion to illustrate the humility and servant role they would need to have going forward. Imagine the reactions of the disciples, who knew Jesus as the Savior, as He began washing their filthy sandal-clad feet following a day of walking the dirt roads of Israel. They were appalled, as shown in Peter's response. *He came to Simon Peter, who said to him, "Lord, are you going to wash my feet?" Jesus replied, "You do not realize now what I am doing, but later you will understand." "No," said Peter, "you shall never wash my feet." Jesus answered, "Unless I wash you, you have no part with me"* (John 13:6-8).

Jesus came *"not to be served but to serve..."* (Matthew 20:28 ESV). As disciples of Jesus, we must be humble servants of others in need. *Now that I, your Lord and Teacher, have washed your feet, you also should wash one another's feet. I have set you an example that you should do as I have done for you. Very truly I tell you, no servant is greater than his master, nor is a messenger greater than the one who sent him* (John 13:14-16).

THE GARDEN OF GETHSEMANE

Following the meal, Jesus and His disciples, less Judas, moved outside to the Garden of Gethsemane to pray. Jesus knew the time was near and He felt the trauma that was about to come as He asked a few of his disciples to stay with Him. *Then he said to them, "My soul is overwhelmed with sorrow to the point of death. Stay here and keep watch with me." Going a little farther, he fell with his face to the ground and prayed, "My Father, if it is possible, may this cup be taken from me. Yet not as I will, but as you will"* (Matthew 26:38-39).

Imagine being Jesus at that moment. He knew everything that had taken place since creation as well as everything that was about to happen. It was neither fair to Jesus nor to the Father who would also suffer for His Son. God was about to do what had to be done to provide the opportunity for all of us to be righteous for eternity in

His presence.

SUFFERING AND DEATH

The fact that Jesus' suffering and death had always been part of God's plan didn't make it any easier. Following the Last Supper, Jesus began suffering in the Garden of Gethsemane. *Then he said to them, "My soul is overwhelmed with sorrow to the point of death* (Matthew 26:38).

Physical punishment soon began and continued throughout His crucifixion. From Isaiah's prophesy we read, *Just as there were many who were appalled at him - his appearance was so disfigured beyond that of any human being and his form marred beyond human likeness* (Isaiah 52:14). We know that other people have suffered torturous deaths and continue to do so today, but there are elements of Jesus' suffering and death that make His like none other.

He had been without sin, shame, and guilt for eternity. Then, suddenly He was experiencing all of the shame, guilt, and wrath of every sin that had been and would be committed by every person to live. That is what Jesus experienced. And if that was not enough, He endured that without the presence of the Father. The wages of every sin were on Him alone. *And at the ninth hour Jesus cried with a loud voice, "Eloi, Eloi, lema sabachthani?" which means, "My God, my God, why have you forsaken me?"* (Mark 15:34 ESV).

While none of us have experienced anything like that, it is a preview of eternal life without God for the many people who refuse to answer His call. People there will experience the shame and guilt of their sins because they refused to accept the gift of Jesus' payment. There will be no turning back and they will live forever in the absence of God and everything good. *For Christ also suffered once for sins, the righteous for the unrighteous, to bring you to God. He was put to death in the body but made alive in the Spirit* (1 Peter 3:18).

THE RESURRECTION

The death and resurrection of Christ are inseparable parts of His salvation mission. Jesus' suffering and death paid for our sins and also destroyed the power of Satan for all who truly believe Christ. *Since the children have flesh and blood, he too shared in their humanity so that by his death he might break the power of him who holds the power of death— that is, the devil— and free those who all their lives were held in slavery by their fear of death* (Hebrews 2:14-15).

The resurrection of Christ Jesus is irrefutable evidence that the devil no longer holds the power of death that was established in the Garden of Eden when man chose to follow Satan. Jesus rose from the dead with a resurrected body, as His true believers will do when Jesus returns to this earth. As true believers, the Spirit of God lives in us, and we are free from the power of sin and death. Jesus said, *"I am the resurrection and the life. The one who believes in me will live, even though they die; and whoever lives by believing in me will never die* (John 11:25-26).

Although that does not make sense to many people, it is understood by people who have been reborn in Christ. *You, however, are not in the realm of the flesh but are in the realm of the Spirit, if indeed the Spirit of God lives in you. And if anyone does not have the Spirit of Christ, they do not belong to Christ. But if Christ is in you, then even though your body is subject to death because of sin, the Spirit gives life because of righteousness. And if the Spirit of him who raised Jesus from the dead is living in you, he who raised Christ from the dead will also give life to your mortal bodies because of his Spirit who lives in you* (Romans 8:9-11).

POST-RESURRECTION APPEARANCES

Following His physical death and resurrection, Jesus appeared to His disciples and others for forty days before ascending to heaven. Given the extensive damage to His body from the crucifixion, we might wonder about His appearance. The Bible tells us that His body was renewed, but He was still recognizable by His friends. Mary Magdalene did not recognize Him at first, but as He spoke to her, there was no doubt that it was Jesus. *Jesus said to her, "Mary." She turned toward him and cried out in Aramaic, "Rabboni!" which means "Teacher"* (John 20:16). Mary then went to the disciples with the news that she had seen the Lord and of course, they were skeptical and still in fear for their lives from the people who had killed Jesus. What happened next tells us a little more about the resurrected body of Jesus. *On the evening of that first day of the week, when the disciples were together, with the doors locked for fear of the Jewish leaders, Jesus came and stood among them and said, "Peace be with you!" After he said this, he showed them his hands and side. The disciples were overjoyed when they saw the Lord* (John 20:19-20). Eight days later, when Thomas was with the disciples, again behind locked doors, Jesus suddenly appeared in the room inviting the doubting Thomas to see and touch His wounds. These appearances and others allowed people to confirm that Jesus had risen from the dead and was quite alive. Jesus used those forty days to prepare His disciples for their role in implementing the next stage of God's plan. *Then Jesus came to them and said, "All authority in heaven and on earth has been given to me. Therefore go and make disciples of all nations, baptizing them in the name of the Father and of the Son and of the Holy Spirit, and teaching them to obey everything I have commanded you. And surely I am with you always, to the very end of the age"* (Matthew 28:18-20).

THE ASCENSION

Jesus' final act on earth was His ascension into heaven in the presence of His disciples, but not before promising another divine resource they would need to fulfill their commission. *On one occasion, while he was eating with them, he gave them this command: "Do not leave Jerusalem, but wait for the gift my Father promised, which you have heard me speak about. For John baptized with water, but in a few days you will be baptized with the Holy Spirit." But you will receive power when the Holy Spirit comes on you; and you will be my witnesses in Jerusalem, and in all Judea and Samaria, and to the ends of the earth." After he said this, he was taken up before their very eyes, and a cloud hid him from their sight* (Acts 1:4-5, 8-9).

Imagine their thoughts at that moment. First of all, what does it mean to be baptized with the Holy Spirit and what kind of power will we have when the Holy Spirit comes upon us? And before they could ask, Jesus was taken up in a cloud before their very eyes! They knew they had a job to do and were about to get help from the Holy Spirit to do it, but they still feared for their lives and went back to Jerusalem as Jesus instructed.

THE RETURN OF JESUS

Jesus' work of salvation was complete, and He returned to heaven with a resurrected body to be at the right hand of God. But God's plan continues because Satan and sin still exist in the world, and God's once-perfect creation continues to decay. It is true that Satan no longer has the power of eternal death, but he still has the power of lies and deceptions to attract unsaved people away from God. The disciples knew they would receive power from the Holy Spirit, but when would they again see Jesus?

Fortunately, two angels immediately appeared to provide the answer. *They were looking intently up into the sky as he was going when suddenly two men dressed in white stood beside them. "Men of Galilee," they said, "why do you stand here looking into the sky? This same Jesus, who has been taken from you into heaven, will come back in the same way you have seen him go into heaven"* (Acts 1:10-11). Jesus was coming back! But when they did not know.

That might have triggered them to recall that Jesus had previously prophesied about end times and His return to earth. *"Therefore keep watch, because you do not know on what day your Lord will come. But understand this: If the owner of the house had known at what time of night the thief was coming, he would have kept watch and would not have let his house be broken into. So you also must be ready, because the Son of Man will come at an hour when you do not expect him* (Matthew 24:42-44).

There was more of God's plan to be revealed, but in the meantime, Jesus provided an extensive improvement plan based on His gift of salvation and power of the Holy Spirit.

A few years later, Paul previewed how Christ Jesus continues to be an integral part of God's plan. *God has now revealed to us his mysterious will regarding Christ—which is to fulfill his own good plan. And this is the plan: At the right time, he will bring everything together under the authority of Christ—everything in heaven and on earth. Furthermore, because we are united with Christ, we have received an inheritance from God, for he chose us in advance, and he makes everything work out according to his plan* (Ephesians 1:9-11 NLT).

DISCUSSION AND REFLECTION

1. We see that as we know the Son of God, we also know the Father. Briefly discuss how that relates to the triune nature of God the Father, God the Son, and God the Holy Spirit. Can you believe that God is three persons in one? Why is that helpful for us to know?

2. Discuss the fact that Jesus has a divine nature and human nature – and yet His human nature is sinless.

3. How does the fact that Jesus called common people to be His apostles relate to our role as His disciples?

4. Read Jesus' Sermon on the Mount and see how He made His points without trying to be politically correct. Find other situations where Jesus took the same approach. See this in light of His reply to Pilate when He said, *"In fact, the reason I was born and came into this world is to testify to the truth"* (John 18:37).

5. Discuss why most of the Jews ultimately turned against Jesus. Relate that to why today's multitudes of lost people are disregarding Jesus rather than allowing Him to be the Lord of their lives.

14. The Holy Spirit

Although Christians believe in the Holy Spirit, along with the Father and Son, many overlook the opportunity and need for a relationship with Him. We learned that it is better for us that Jesus returned to heaven because the Father would then send the Holy Spirit to us in another way. Now we learn how the Holy Spirit helps us to know God, give glory to Him and follow Jesus as a disciple.

Jesus says the Holy Spirit is our advocate to the Father and our communication link with Him. Because the Holy Spirit is simultaneously in the heart of every true believer, Jesus is also with every person who receives Him as Savior and Lord. *"If you love me, keep my commands. And I will ask the Father, and he will give you another advocate to help you and be with you forever— the Spirit of truth. The world cannot accept him, because it neither sees him nor knows him. But you know him, for he lives with you and will be in you. I will not leave you as orphans; I will come to you. Before long, the world will not see me anymore, but you will see me. Because I live, you also will live (John 14:15-19). But when he, the Spirit of truth, comes, he will guide you into all the truth. He will not speak on his own; he will speak only what he hears, and he will tell you what is yet to come. He will glorify me because it is from me that he will receive what he will make known to you (John 16:13-14). So,* how do we relate to the Holy Spirit in those ways?

FIRST

The Holy Spirit first comes to us at the moment we truly believe and receive Jesus as our Savior and Lord. In John 14:17, Jesus reminds His true believers, *"But you know him* (the Holy Spirit), *for he lives with you..."* My analogy is that our gift of salvation provides us with a new life and new genetic makeup that we never had before. Just as genes are units of heredity transferred from a parent to offspring, the Holy Spirit is like the heredity of God transferred to each true believer. In effect, at the moment we are born again in Christ, we receive the Holy Spirit as a genetic link to the Father and Son, and we are then members of His eternal family. In this way, the Holy Spirit remains with us to communicate on our behalf with the Father and Son.

GROW IN THE SPIRIT

As newly created persons in Christ, we desire to grow and mature spiritually and become the masterpieces that God created us to be, but we cannot do that without the Holy Spirit. As our advocate, the Holy Spirit communicates with the Father and Son and back to us from them. As Jesus said, *"But when he, the Spirit of truth, comes, he will guide you into all the truth. He will not speak on his own; he will speak only what he hears, and he will tell you what is yet to come"* (John 16:13). The Holy Spirit allows Jesus to be with each of us as our life-coach. In this way, each believer has a personal relationship with God the Father, the Son and the Holy Spirit, allowing us to grow and mature as true believers.

We know that Paul dropped out of his previous life, immediately following his salvation experience on the road to Damascus. As a new creation, Paul allowed Jesus, through the Holy Spirit, to mature him to the point where he was ready to go into the world and make a difference for the glory of God. During those three years, Paul grew to know the one true God and find freedom from the strongholds of his past life. He also listened to Jesus to learn his purpose and role for his new life going forward. By the time he rejoined the world, Paul had a clear vision of what Jesus would lead him to do for the remainder of his life on earth. Although we may not go into seclusion in that same way to mature spiritually, we must be intentional and allow that to happen with the power of the Holy Spirit.

THE POWER OF THE SPIRIT

In addition to helping us grow and mature in our knowledge of the truth and our relationship with God, the Holy Spirit also provides supernatural power to us to do the will of God. There can be special situations when the Holy Spirit works in us and through us to do things we could not otherwise do. These supernatural powers can occur in our lives as true believers today, as seen in the lives of the first-generation disciples.

Before he rose back to heaven, Jesus spoke to His close followers who were already true believers. *On one occasion, while he was eating with them, he gave them this command: "Do not leave Jerusalem, but wait for the gift my Father promised, which you have heard me speak about. For John baptized with water, but in a few days, you will be baptized with the Holy Spirit"* (Acts 1:4-5). Then soon after that and immediately before rising to heaven, Jesus told them: *But you will receive power when the Holy Spirit comes on you...* (v. 8).

At that point, the apostles and other disciples were aware that the Holy Spirit was already with them since their moment of salvation, but they were still paralyzed with fear because Jesus was gone. They were afraid because they had a commission to make disciples among the same people who had crucified Jesus only a few weeks earlier. Then it happened: *When the day of Pentecost came, they were all together in one place. Suddenly a sound like the blowing of a violent wind came from heaven and filled the whole house where they were sitting. They saw what seemed to be tongues of fire that separated and came to rest on each of them. All of them were filled with the Holy Spirit and began to speak in other tongues as the Spirit enabled them* (Acts 2:1-4). When the Holy Spirit descended upon them, they were empowered with supernatural strength and new abilities to begin their commission to make disciples.

With the power and direction of the Holy Spirit, they boldly and effectively witnessed in the name of Jesus as Savior and Lord. *Then Peter stood up with the Eleven, raised his voice and addressed the crowd: "Fellow Jews and all of you who live in Jerusalem, let me explain this to you; listen carefully to what I say... With many other words he warned them; and he pleaded with them, "Save yourselves from this corrupt generation." Those who accepted his message were baptized, and about three thousand were added to their number that day* (Acts 2:14-41).

We, too, can be blessed with supernatural power from the Holy Spirit to do the will of God. As we prepare to go into the world to make a difference, we should pray for and look for opportunities to make disciples and provide glory and honor to God. When needed, the power of the Holy Spirit will come upon us to do things that we could not do without Him. In between those times, the Holy Spirit continues as our advocate with the Father and Son.

FRUIT OF THE SPIRIT

The fact is that some true Christians are initially reluctant to invite the supernatural power of the Holy Spirit into their lives. They admire disciples like Paul and other people today who give everything to be His witness, but they do not see themselves in that role. Of course, God tells us that making disciples requires a team effort. *The Spirit's presence is shown in some way in each person for the good of all (1 Corinthians 12:7 GNT).* The presence of the Holy Spirit allows us to be the people that God wants us to be, and that gives us joy beyond anything we can attain on our own.

After receiving the Holy Spirit, Paul experienced life with Jesus as his Lord. God's plan for him was to plant the seed of Christianity beyond the small culture of the Jewish people, and we thank God for that today. Paul experienced plenty of opposition and hardship along the way, but his view of life with the Holy Spirit was very encouraging. *But the Holy Spirit produces this kind of fruit in our lives: love, joy, peace, patience, kindness, goodness, faithfulness, gentleness, and self-control. There is no law against these things!* (Galatians 5:22-23). This list of Spirit-filled qualities is known as the Fruit of the Spirit, and Paul's writings show us how he experienced this fruit as he pursued his calling and ministry.

FINISHING THE RACE

Following his conversion, Paul went all-in to live God's way, allowing the Holy Spirit to work with him and in him to do the extraordinary things that all of us benefit from today. He valued his life in Christ and looked forward to the rewards to come. *I have fought the good fight, I have finished the race, I have kept the faith. Now there is in store for me the crown of righteousness, which the Lord, the righteous Judge, will award to me on that day—and not only to me, but also to all who have longed for his appearing* (2 Timothy 4:7-8).

With Jesus as our Lord, we too have that confidence and peace. The Holy Spirit is with us, providing the direction and power we need. We may not see our role as grand as Paul's, but we are part of Jesus' team of disciples commissioned to give God glory by making disciples. Because the enemy is working against us, we need the Holy Spirit. We cannot resist the enemy and be disciples of Jesus with only our efforts, but we can win that fight with the power of the Holy Spirit, who overcomes all the challenges we face in this life. We must turn to Him and trust in His help. We make the unqualified commitment, and God provides the resources and path forward for our life on earth with eternal rewards to follow.

DISCUSSION AND REFLECTION

1. Discuss your understanding of the Holy Spirit. Why is the Holy Spirit so important to our peace, joy, and growth following our Salvation experience?

2. How does the Holy Spirit come into play as we are drawn to build our personal relationship with Jesus as Lord of our lives?

3. Describe other ways that the Holy Spirit helps us to live according to God's purpose and will.

15. God's Plan Fulfilled

" Here I am! I stand at the door and knock. If anyone hears my voice and opens the door, I will come in and eat with that person, and they with me. To the one who is victorious, I will give the right to sit with me on my throne, just as I was victorious and sat down with my Father on his throne" (Revelation 3:20-21).

What an invitation to be known by Jesus and live with Him for eternity! He calls us to open the door of our heart and invite Him to make us a new creation. With that rebirth, we receive the assurance of our eternal destiny with God, and we enjoy His divine presence in this life. At the same time, I still look forward to those days in heaven when Jesus shows up at my door to dine with me – a leisurely meal with a best friend and conversation that flows with ease, humor, and love.

EVERYTHING NEW AND RIGHT

I heard a loud shout from the throne, saying, "Look, God's home is now among his people! He will live with them, and they will be his people. God himself will be with them. He will wipe every tear from their eyes, and there will be no more death or sorrow or crying or pain. All these things are gone forever." And the one sitting on the throne said, "Look, I am making everything new!" (Revelation 21:3-

5 NLT).

Everything new! We will have new glorified bodies and live on a new perfect earth, and for the first time, we will be the masterpiece creations that God intended us to be. *And just as we have borne the likeness of the earthly man, so shall we bear the likeness of the man from heaven* (1 Corinthians 15:49). Our glorified bodies will be united with our spirits and souls and be forever free from the curse of sin (1 Corinthians 15:42-44, 51-53).

We will be united with family and friends who are part of God's adopted family and have the opportunity to fellowship with others who are living for the glory of God. The enemy will be gone, along with all people who chose not to believe and receive Jesus as Savior and Lord. There will be no evil, no crime, no pain, no sickness, no sadness, no shame, no depression, no need for forgiveness, no bitterness, no rejection, no fear, no revenge, no guilt, no hate, no insults, no anger, no sadness, no abuse, no betrayal, no humiliation, no persecution, no blame, and no sad memories of this fallen world – it is life as God created it to be. We will be living according to God's plan, and it will be *very good.*

REWARDS

As true believers of Jesus, we will receive rewards for the good we are doing today on our Narrow Road journey – for our generosity, service and love for others. *"Look, I am coming soon! My reward is with me, and I will give to each person according to what they have done"* (Revelation 22:12). We will be rewarded with opportunities and responsibilities based on how we handle our God-given responsibilities now. *"Well done, good and faithful servant! You have been faithful with a few things; I will put you in charge of many things. Come and share your master's happiness!"* (Matthew 25:23).

We will appreciate the perfection of God's plan for our new lives, and we will be happy as we fellowship with Him and other believers. We will be giving glory to God in heaven and living as God designed life to be lived – and it won't be boring!

ENCOURAGEMENT NOW

So, as we travel the Narrow Road among the billions of lost people and the enemy who continues to lie and deceive people into evil, it's comforting to know there is much more to life than the life we know today. *Now we live with great expectation, and we have a priceless inheritance—an inheritance that is kept in heaven for you, pure and undefiled, beyond the reach of change and decay. And through your faith, God is protecting you by his power until you receive this salvation, which is ready to be revealed on the last day for all to see* (1 Peter 1:3-5 NLT).

THY KINGDOM COME...

And we do not have to wait. Heaven awaits us, but in the meantime, Jesus tells us to pray for His kingdom to come on earth and for God's will to be done today as we complete this earthly journey. That can happen because Heaven is more than a destination – it is our all-in relationship with the Father, the Son, and the Holy Spirit, along with God's family of true believers. We grow in those God-blessed relationships as we allow Jesus to be the Lord of our lives. We discover our role in His purpose to glorify God and lead others to do the same. I pray, Father, that Your kingdom will come and Your will be done in our lives on earth, as I am sure it will be in Heaven. Amen.

DISCUSSION AND REFLECTION

1. Think about Jesus' invitation in Revelation 3:20-12 to personally dine with us. Can you see your relationship with Him

growing in this earthly life to the point where you are experiencing His presence to that extent? Do you want to have that, or are you still wanting your way now and His way later?

2. If you want that relationship now, spend time in prayer communication with God and submit to Jesus to be the Lord of your life going forward. You can discuss this, but also spend personal time with God on this.

3. Although we are promised eternal rewards for the good works we do as disciples of Jesus, why are rewards not the real motivation as we follow Jesus as our Lord? What is our motivation?

4. Can you see that living for the honor and glory of God, and allowing Him to lead us in everything we do, is His plan for our lives? What are your next steps to encourage that happen?

Afterword

Yes, we can be assured that Jesus recognizes us as a believer and adopted member of His eternal family. The Word of God tells us how we can know Jesus will be welcoming us with open arms when we eventually meet Him at the time of His prophesy in Matthew 7:21-23.

From the moment we truly believe and receive Jesus as Savior and Lord, we begin a new life in Christ, and we grow toward His perfection. Even if we pass away from this life at that moment, Jesus welcomes us to Heaven. We are adopted into the eternal family of God, just as the thief on the cross with Jesus. However, most of us have more time on this earth to grow and mature in our new life, and the Word of God provides indicators of our new life in Christ.

Because our heart and spirit are changed with our new life in Christ, the thoughts we have and the things we do and say begin to reflect the presence of the Holy Spirit within us. In Matthew 7, Jesus tells us that His followers are recognized by the fruit of their life. He says: "*A good tree cannot bear bad fruit, and a bad tree cannot bear good fruit* (Matthew 7:18). That is not to say we become perfect at the moment of our new life in Christ, but we intentionally work toward His perfection as we submit to Him as Lord and King of our life. The Word of God describes some ways for us to know that we are growing and maturing in our relationship with the one true God:

> ✟ **We trust in the Lord** – In our heart, we completely trust that Jesus' death and resurrection paid the wages of our sin throughout all of our life. We believe that nothing we do could pay the price needed to give us new life in Christ. *For*

it is by grace you have been saved, through faith—and this is not from yourselves, it is the gift of God—not by works, so that no one can boast (Ephesians 2:8-9).

✞ **We commit to Jesus as Lord of our life** – Our heartfelt decision to believe and receive Jesus includes our commitment to follow Jesus as Lord of our life going forward. In other words, we cannot accept Jesus to ensure Heaven and then intentionally live the remainder of our earthly life without Him as Lord. Believing and receiving Jesus means receiving Him as Lord of our life going forward. Sometimes we falter amid this fallen world, but our commitment to Jesus as Lord is never in question. *No one who is born of God will continue to sin, because God's seed remains in them; they cannot go on sinning, because they have been born of God* (1 John 3:9). *Then he said to them all: "Whoever wants to be my disciple must deny themselves and take up their cross daily and follow me* (Luke 9:23).

✞ **We depend on the one true God** – This means we grow to know the truth of who He is. We turn to Him as the Father, Son and Holy Spirit, to the truth of His Word, and to His family of true believers. *But now that you have been set free from sin and have become slaves of God, the benefit you reap leads to holiness, and the result is eternal life* (Romans 6:22).

✞ **We love God and love our neighbors** – Jesus summarizes all of the commandments Matthew 22:37-39. We cannot do that with only our efforts; we need to trust in the Lord as Lord and utilize all of the divine resources He provides to us. *We know that we have passed from death to life, because* *we love each other. Anyone who does not love remains in death* (1 John 3:14). *By this everyone will know that you are my disciples, if you love one another* (John 13:35).

✝ **We accept God's purpose for us** - We live for the glory of God and pursue Jesus' commission to make disciples. Our new life has a new purpose. *But grow in the grace and knowledge of our Lord and Savior Jesus Christ. To him be glory both now and forever! Amen* (2 Peter 3:18).

Acknowledgements

At least in my case, it took a team effort to get me from being an assumed Christian, sixteen years ago, to writing this book today. For the most part, these people don't know each other and some of them didn't even know me. My gratitude and acknowledgments extend from the person who introduced me to the Proverbs 3:5-6 verse, to the people who encouraged me to see beyond my assumptions, to people who likely prayed for me, to Jesus who carried me through the Narrow Gate onto the Narrow Road to life, to my family and friends who accepted and welcomed me into my new life, to the writers and pastors who helped me mature spiritually, and to the people who helped me compose and edit this book. I now see this as part of God's plan and approach for making disciples. Jesus calls the plays and the Holy Spirit provides the communication and power for His disciples to make it happen – and I am now forever blessed to be part of His team.

And looking forward, I am encouraged by the words of this song:

> Behold I have a friend
> The Spirit breathing holy fire within
> My ever-present help
> Speaking truth when I can't find it
> Light up this broken heart
> And light my way
> Until my time on earth is done
> Oh Holy Spirit
> Breathe in me like kingdom come
> Oh Holy Spirit
> Let Your work in me be done
>
> *Behold Then Sings My Soul*; Hillsong Worship.
> Words and music by Joel Houston.

Notes

INTRODUCTION

Population and religion information is from: "The Future of World Religions: Population Growth Projections 2010-2050," Pew Research Center, April 2, 2015, https://www.pewforum.org/2015/04/02/religious-projections-2010-2050/.

Chapter 3 – TRUTH

My initial interest in the topic of 'truth' came from Focus on the Family's production of The Truth Project (https://www.focusonthefamily.com/faith/the-truth-project/). This video-based home Bible study is a starting point for looking at life from a biblical perspective. The opening question in this Truth chapter where Pilate sarcastically asks: "What is truth?" is presented by Del Tackett. Another of his intriguing arguments is what Jesus could have said as the reason He came into this world.

Additional understanding of the topics of 'truth' and 'relativism' came from John Piper (https://www.desiringgod.org/). Two specific articles are: 'Jesus Came into the World to Bear Witness to the Truth' (https://www.desiringgod.org/messages/jesus-came-into-the-world-to-bear-witness-to-the-truth); and 'Challenging the Church and Culture with Truth' (https://www.desiringgod.org/messages/challenging-the-church-and-culture-with-truth).

The Barna Group has been conducting and analyzing primary research to understand cultural trends related to values, beliefs, attitudes and behaviors since 1984. The information referenced under the Relativism heading comes from: https://www.barna.com/research/competing-worldviews-influence-todays-christians/.

Regarding the topic of the Holy Bible and truth, two sources provide a good argument for its credibility as the Word of God. 'Why You Can Believe the Bible' is found in the EveryStudent.com website (https://www.everystudent.com/features/bible.html); and two articles are from GotQuestions.org (https://www.gotquestions.org/Bible-God-Word.html and https://www.gotquestions.org/proof-inspiration-Bible.html).

Chapter 4 – THE RELATIONSHIP

Just As I Am, Without One Plea. Hymn authored by Charlotte Elliott. First published in 1649. Source: https://www.hymnary.org

Part 3: A NEW LIFE

The list of strongholds is from: Beth Moore, *Praying God's Word,* (Nashville, TN.; B&H Publishing Group, 2009). Each stronghold is explained related to prayers and verses from the Bible.

Chapter 9 – MAKING IT HAPPEN

The essence of this chapter comes from what I have learned over the past few years at Church of the Highlands (https://www.churchofthehighlands.com/). The ongoing theme is to Know God, Find Freedom, Discover Purpose and Make a Difference, along with the overriding message to Pray First. [Chris Hodges, *What's Next: The Journey to Know God, Find Freedom, Discover Purpose & Make a Difference.* (Nashville, TN: Nelson Books, 2019)].

5 Powerful Components to the Lord's Prayer, Larry Stockstill, provides a concise explanation of this prayer template. (https://www.larrystockstill.com/blog/prayer-template).

Chapter 10 – THE ONE TRUE GOD

Background for the list of attributes of the one true God include the Bright Media Foundation (http://www.brightmedia.org/), and a specific article entitled 'Discover God's Attributes' (https://www.josh.org/wp-content/uploads/PDF/resources-josh_talks attributes_of_god.pdf).

Chapter 14 – THE HOLY SPIRIT

John Piper (www.desiringgod.org) was my primary source for clarity on the topic of the Holy Spirit. He has several archived articles including this one that especially spoke to me: What Is the Baptism of the Holy Spirit? (https://www.desiringgod.org/interviews/what-is-the-baptism-of-the-holy-spirit).

Chapter 15 – GOD'S PLAN FULFILLED

"There is much more to life than this life" is a frequent quote from Pastor Chris Hodges, Church of the Highlands.

About The Author

Al Sikes, who continues to be an average guy for seven decades, uses the pen name, A.D. Sikes. He has been writing for the past sixteen years and has three books that focus on the theme of assumed Christianity. Al continues to write on that topic because he is still amazed that he lived fifty-five years under the assumption he was good with God. Not until he went all-in to believe and receive Jesus did he realize what he had been missing. As he says, "I didn't know what I didn't know."

With an engineering degree and advanced business studies, Al's first career was in the electric power industry, followed by a management consulting practice for the last 25 years of his professional career. He continues to be involved in that to a limited extent, but his focus now is to help lost people know what they are missing. He is doing that and enjoying life with his wife of nearly fifty years, along with their two daughters, their husbands, and six grandchildren.

Other Books by A.D. Sikes

- *Jack, The Assumed Christian* – The fictional story about a guy named Jack who was invited by God to ask one question which was answered each night in his dream. Copyright 2006. (Rewritten as *AWAKE to a New Life…*)

- *My Way Take 2* – The author's story of living My Way like the song originally sung by Frank Sinatra. Copyright 2018.

I welcome your comments and story:

al@assumedchristianity.com

https://assumedchristianity.com/

www.ingramcontent.com/pod-product-compliance
Lightning Source LLC
Chambersburg PA
CBHW031623040426
42452CB00007B/652

9781734038408